VEGETARIAN
SHEET PAN COOKING

VEGETARIAN
SHEET PAN COOKING

101 recipes for simple and nutritious meat-free meals straight from the oven

LIZ FRANKLIN

Photography by Steve Painter

RYLAND PETERS & SMALL
LONDON • NEW YORK

First published in 2018 by
Ryland Peters & Small
20–21 Jockey's Fields, London
WC1R 4BW
and 341 E 116th St, New York NY 10029
www.rylandpeters.com

10 9 8 7 6 5 4 3 2 1

ISBN: 978-1-78879-029-1

Printed in China

Notes:
• Both British (Metric) and American
(Imperial plus US cups) measurements
are included in these recipes for your
convenience, however it is important to work
with one set of measurements only and not
alternate between the two within a recipe.
• All spoon measurements are level unless
otherwise specified. A teaspoon is 5 ml,
a tablespoon is 15 ml.
• All eggs are medium (UK) or large (US),
unless specified as large, in which case
US extra-large should be used. Uncooked
or partially cooked eggs should not be
served to the very old, frail, young children,
pregnant women or those with compromised
immune systems.
• Ovens should be preheated to the
specified temperatures. We recommend
using an oven thermometer. If using a
fan-assisted oven, adjust temperatures
according to the manufacturer's instructions.

For Matilda Joyce
the newest, most gorgeous
and giggliest member of
the family with all the love
in the universe xxx

Senior designer Toni Kay
Editor Miriam Catley
Production controller
  Mai-Ling Collyer
Art director Leslie Harrington
Editorial director Julia Charles
Publisher Cindy Richards

Photography & prop styling
  Steve Painter
Food stylist Lucy McKelvie
Indexer Vanessa Bird

CONTENTS

INTRODUCTION

For many years, I tested and reviewed equipment and gadgets for a very well known high street retailer of kitchenware. Some of the implements and appliances I tested were really useful, some not so much, but at the end of the day, I found very few truly indispensable items. Most ended up at the back of a cupboard, packed off to the charity shop, or given away to friends (who probably now have them at the back of their cupboards). Conversely, a handful of simple essentials have stood the test of time and I've come to appreciate them more and more as the years have gone by – a good set of knives, some sturdy stainless steel saucepans – and a set of really robust roasting/sheet pans.

Once upon a time, the roasting pan might have been considered second fiddle to the all-important saucepan. The oven was reserved largely for cooking bread and other baked edibles, and for roasting meat, poultry and roast potatoes. Delicious and appreciated though these favourites were and still are, all manner of the truly scrumptious can be created when oven and sheet pan conspire. What makes the collaboration even more tempting, is that this magic can be achieved using just one sheet pan, and so the stack of dirty dishes heading for the sink is kept to an encouraging minimum. This fact in itself can help the whole business of making a meal much quicker to prepare and therefore less stressful – but the bottom line is that the results are utterly incredible! In short, what's absolutely not to love about a way of cooking that is super-convenient, really relaxing, easy on the washing up and big on flavour?

When the lovely Julia Charles asked me to write this book, I couldn't have been more thrilled; it combines so many of the food related things that I'm crazy about. As a once very strict vegetarian, I have long been a fan of loading up a pan with vegetables, pulses, grains and other goodies, throwing them in the oven and leaving them to look after themselves, and so the idea of a book concentrating on vegetarian and vegan recipes oven-cooked on a single sheet pan was something I couldn't wait to get to work on.

Plant-based diets have never been more popular. Once considered a simple support act to a meat or fish dish, the vegetable is now the rising star – a fact now acknowledged by many of the world's top restaurants. French chef Alain Passard has declared this 'the golden age of vegetables' and centres the whole menu at his Michelin 3 Star restaurant Arpege around the vegetables grown in the eatery's gardens. At the height of my journey through serious vegetarianism, I was very much in the minority – eating out at even the best restaurants often resulted in the same old boring offer – a dry and dreary nut cutlet that had all the appeal of eating a chunk of old carpet. Now, as global issues highlight food related scares and scandals, we are all becoming far more aware of the animal cruelty involved in intensive farming methods, antibiotic resistance, the growing occurrence of lice infestation in farmed fish, and the huge implications of greenhouse gas emissions arising from the methane production that supports many of these systems. We hear regular reports from health experts on the probable link between over consumption of some animal products and disease, so there is little wonder that more and more of us are cutting out animal protein and products from our diets, or at very least reducing them.

The great thing is that we now have access to such a superabundance of wonderful, versatile and healthy vegetables and fresh herbs, and increasing numbers of us are growing our own as the popularity of allotments rises. We can easily shop for amazing spices and ingredients from around the world, and there are so many good things to provide the protein element of our meal without having to cook meat or fish.

Some of the recipes that follow are built on a bedrock of roasted vegetables and fruit. Heat from the oven helps to release the natural sugars in them and gives a glorious depth of flavour. Depending on what's being cooked – there's often a bonus of crispy edges. But there are recipes for things you might not associate with oven cooking too – glorious soups, fabulous fritters, and the best ever

baked porridge. There are savouries to tempt, sugary treats to try – all bound up with inspiration from around the world. From Ethiopian Lentil Casserole, to Tex-Mex Vegetable Tacos with Chipotle Mayonnaise. From Salt Baked Celeriac with Blue Cheese and Honey-glazed Treviso to Cauliflower, Mango and Sultana Salad. Sweet Treats include Bay-scented Hasselback Orchard Fruits and Coconut Macaroon Queen of Puddings, with its billowing meringue crown. There are recipes to start the day, and even some to snack on.

Whether you are a long-time vegetarian or vegan, entertaining friends or family who may be following a plant-based diet, or simply trying to cut down on your intake of meat and fish – the following pages offer a whole host of tempting dishes to try. I hope you enjoy making and sharing them every bit as much as I have loved bringing them to life.

A Note on Sheet Pans
If there is one thing that I have learned from many years cooking both professionally and for family and friends, it is, without a shred of doubt, that buying good, solid sheet pans/ roasting tins and looking after them will serve you well and save you money in the long run. Cheap ones will only buckle and possibly even rust. Over the course of the book, I have used three different sizes – all heavy duty carbon steel, and non stick – a large, flat sheet pan/

roasting tray measuring 35 x 25 x 2 cm/ 13¾ x 9 x ¾ inches, a slightly smaller but deeper one measuring 30 x 23 x 5 cm/ 12 x 9 x 2 inches and a brownie pan sized 30 x 17 x 2.5 cm/11¾ x 6¾ x 1 inch and they have all been worth their weight in gold.

Storecupboard stars

The benefits of keeping a well-stocked storecupboard should never be underestimated – with quality always taking precedence over quantity. Better to keep small supplies of really great ingredients you'll turn to time and time again than stockpile industrial quantities of things you won't get to use before they're stale and flavourless. The best kind of storecupboard should be one that naturally calls to be restocked regularly as it's built on items you love to use almost every day. That way, you'll find that you can always rustle up something for supper if you've had an especially busy day, or have unexpected mouths to feed.

Bottles

Oil – Unless otherwise stated, I have used extra virgin olive oil in the recipes throughout the book. It's healthy, made from just one ingredient and, contrary to popular myth, can be heated to quite high temperatures. Buy a blended one for cooking, and something a little more special for drizzling and dressing. A bottle each of balsamic, red and white wine vinegar are all invaluable and I always keep sherry vinegar, rice wine vinegar and apple cider vinegar too. Also, soy sauce (dark and sweet Indonesian kejap manis), sriracha sauce (addictive) and good quality tomato ketchup.

Jars

Tahini, miso paste, palm-oil free nut butters (peanut, almond, cashew) wholegrain and Dijon mustards, passata/strained tomatoes, maple syrup, date syrup, and brown rice syrup are all valuable for a plant-based storecupboard. Dried spices and peppers are worth their weight in gold, but don't buy in bulk unless you're really going to use big quantities.

Cans

Coconut milk, chopped tomatoes, pulses/ legumes (such as chickpeas, lentils and various beans) are all such useful ingredients to fall back on.

Packets

Salt flakes, pasta, rice (basmati, carnaroli), jumbo oats, spelt flakes, pulses/legumes and grains, nuts and seeds (keep these in the fridge though), nutritional yeast flakes.

In the fridge

For vegans, plant-based yogurts are indispensable. Nut and oat milks are delicious and versatile. Store fresh herbs in your fridge wrapped in slightly dampened paper towels to help keep them fresh for longer. And keep pots of fresh herbs on the windowsill ready to pick and add to your cooking, always!

BREAKFAST & BRUNCH

SLOW-BAKED PECAN & COCOA NIB GRANOLA
WITH GOJI & GOLDEN BERRIES

Long, slow-baking gives granola a lovely flavour and crunchy texture, making this an absolute winner (and much cheaper than store-bought). Adding an egg white to the mixture helps the oats and seeds stick together in little clusters, but if you'd prefer it to be vegan-friendly, then simply leave the egg white out – the texture will just be a little more free-flowing.

Serve it with a good dollop of your favourite natural or coconut yogurt and some fresh fruit, adding a drizzle of honey or date syrup if you fancy a little extra sweetness.

250 g/2½ cups jumbo oats
100 g/¾ cup mixed seeds
   (sunflower, hemp, sesame,
   linseed, chia, etc.)
50 g/1¾ oz. coconut oil
   (or substitute olive oil)
50 ml/3½ tbsp brown rice syrup
a pinch of salt

1 egg white, lightly whisked
150 g/scant 1½ cups pecans,
   roughly chopped
100 g/3½ oz. golden berries
100 g/3½ oz. goji berries
50 g/1¾ oz. cocoa nibs

MAKES 10

Preheat the oven to 150°C (300°F) Gas 2. Put the oats and seeds into a bowl and grate in the coconut oil (or add the olive oil). Add the brown rice syrup and salt. Stir until evenly mixed. Add the egg white and mix through until the oats are coated and the mix is forming little clusters. Spread over a roasting pan and bake for about 40 minutes, until the granola is golden and crisp. Add the pecans and return to the oven for a further 5–10 minutes, until the nuts are lightly toasted. Remove from the oven and leave to cool before stirring in the berries and cocoa nibs. Store in an airtight container.

CRANBERRY BREAKFAST BARS

So these crunchy, fruity, seed-packed bars are perfect as a treat for breakfast on the move. They're great to tuck into a lunch box too. Do please make sure to use 'jumbo' oats, rather than the fluffier 'rolled' porridge oats, or the bars won't have such a moist and moreish texture. Look out for good-quality, plump juicy cranberries too.

180 g/1½ sticks butter, melted
180 g/1 cup minus 1⅓ tbsp
   light muscovado sugar
50 g/scant ¼ cup runny honey
200 g/2 cups jumbo oats
200 g/2 cups cornflakes
100 g/¾ cup mixed seeds
   (pumpkin, sunflower, chia,
   linseed, sesame, etc.)

100 g/¾ cup plump dried
   cranberries

a 30 x 17 x 2.5 cm/
   11¾ x 6¾ x 1 inch brownie
   pan, lightly greased and lined
   with baking parchment

MAKES 12–15

Preheat the oven to 180°C (350°F) Gas 4. Put the melted butter, muscovado sugar and honey together in a large bowl and stir until evenly mixed. Add the oats, cornflakes, seeds and cranberries, and mix until everything is evenly incorporated. Spoon the mixture into the prepared pan and bake for 20–25 minutes, until the mixture is golden brown and firm.

Leave in the pan to cool, and then cut into squares. Store in an airtight tin.

ROAST RHUBARB, BLACKBERRY & BLUEBERRY COMPOTE
WITH COCONUT YOGURT

This three-fruit combo tastes every bit as lovely as it looks. Oven-roasting is a perfect way to cook rhubarb – it keeps its shape nicely (so long as you don't overcook it and scoop a little too hard to get it out of the pan). A generous trickle of Grenadine is an optional extra, but it will add the prettiest pink blush to the juices – it's a lovely ruby red syrup made out of pomegranate seeds (although do look out for the Real McCoy, as the cheaper, almost fluorescent brands are often just a mixture of corn syrup and colouring).

400 g/14 oz. rhubarb
200 g/1½ cups blackberries
200 g/1½ cups blueberries
60 g/2¼ oz. caster/granulated sugar
60 ml/¼ cup boiling water
seeds from 2 vanilla pods
50 ml/3½ tbsp Grenadine (optional)
400 g/scant 2 cups coconut yogurt,
   to serve

SERVES 4

Preheat the oven to 190°C (375°F) Gas 5. Trim the rhubarb and remove any stringy bits. Cut the stalks into 3 cm/1¼ inch lengths and arrange on a large, deep sheet pan. Scatter over the blackberries and blueberries. Mix the sugar and boiling water together in a jug and add the seeds from the vanilla pods. Stir in the Grenadine (if using) and pour the mixture over the fruit in the pan. Cover with foil and roast for about 12–15 minutes, until the rhubarb is just soft. Remove from the oven and serve warm, with the coconut yogurt.

BAKED OAT MILK PORRIDGE
WITH PEARS, ALMONDS & DATE SYRUP

160 g/1¾ cups jumbo oats
1.2 litres/5 cups oat milk
75 g/½ cup mixed seeds
2 tsp vanilla bean paste
1 tsp ground cinnamon
3 medium ripe, but firm pears,
    cored and diced
80 g/⅔ cup mixed dried berries
    (sultanas/golden raisins, goji berries,
    golden berries, cranberries, etc.)

to serve
2 tbsp toasted flaked/slivered almonds
4–5 tbsp date syrup
extra oat milk

SERVES 4-6

You might wonder why on earth anyone would want to oven-bake porridge, when it takes so little time to cook the conventional way? Well, it does mean that you can swap standing at the hob and stirring constantly for simply mixing everything together and leaving it to morph into breakfast heaven under its own steam, while you soak in the bath, practice your sun salutations, get ready for work, or even go back to bed with your book!

Preheat the oven to 170°C (325°F) Gas 3. Mix the oats and oat milk together. Stir in the seeds, vanilla bean paste, ground cinnamon, diced pears and dried berries. Pour everything into a roasting pan, cover with foil and bake for 30 minutes. Remove from the oven and spoon into bowls. Scatter with the toasted almonds and drizzle with date syrup and extra oat milk as desired. Serve at once.

POLENTA PORRIDGE WITH STEM GINGER,
WALNUTS & ROASTED BLACKBERRY JAM

Polenta/cornmeal is a complex carbohydrate, releasing energy slowly into the body and thus keeping you feeling fuller for longer. Here it's topped with a glorious, inky, roasted berry jam and slivers of shiny stem ginger, but it's fabulous with freshly chopped fruit or a compote too.

150 g/1 cup quick-cook polenta/cornmeal
1 litre/4 cups plus 3 tbsp almond, oat or
    cow's milk, plus extra to serve
1 tbsp caster/granulated sugar
5–6 nuggets stem ginger, thinly sliced
a handful of chopped walnuts

for the roasted berry jam
800 g/28 oz. caster/granulated sugar
800 g/8 cups mixed blackberries,
    redcurrants, blackcurrants, etc.

SERVES 4

Preheat the oven to 180°C (350°F) Gas 4. Put the polenta/cornmeal into a deep sheet pan and slowly pour in your chosen milk, stirring until the mixture is smooth. Stir in the sugar, cover with foil and bake for about 25 minutes or so, until the porridge is thickened and cooked. Top with autumn berry jam, slices of stem ginger (pour a little of the syrup from the jar on too), and chopped walnuts. Add an extra drizzle of your chosen milk too, if desired.

ROASTED BERRY JAM
Preheat the oven to 180°C (350°F) Gas 4. Scatter the sugar over the base of a roasting pan, cover with foil and pop it in the oven for about 15–20 minutes, to warm the sugar. Remove from the oven and stir in the fruit. Re-cover the fruit and roast for a further 45–50 minutes or so, until the jam is thick and glossy. Cool, cover and store in the fridge (in a bowl) for up to a week – or spoon into sterilized jars, seal and store for up to a month in the fridge.

BAY-SCENTED COCONUT MILK BLACK RICE WITH TROPICAL FRUITS

I can't tell you how good the combination of lightly sweetened chewy black rice and coconut milk is – but it does need that pinch of salt flakes to bring everything together, so please don't be tempted to skip it.

3 x 400-ml/14-fl. oz. cans coconut milk
250 g/scant 1½ cups riso venere black rice
50 g/¼ cup caster/granulated sugar
a pinch of salt flakes
2 bay leaves

to serve
1 ripe papaya
½ medium ripe pineapple
1 ripe mango
2 kiwi fruit
2–3 passion fruit

SERVES 4

Preheat the oven to 170°C (325°F) Gas 3. Pour the coconut milk into a large bowl, fill up one of the cans with water and add this, and then stir in the rice, sugar and salt flakes. Transfer the mixture into a roasting pan and add in the bay leaves. Cover the pan with foil and bake for about 1¼ hours, until the rice is soft and chewy, but not dry. Peel, then cut the papaya in half, remove the seeds and cut into slices. Peel the pineapple, remove the hard core and cut into chunks. Peel the mango, remove the stone and cut into slices. Peel and slice the kiwi fruit. Cut the passion fruit into halves. Remove the bay leaves from the rice, give it a stir and serve in bowls, topped with the fruit and a drizzle of passion fruit pulp.

BROWN RICE, QUINOA & CHIA BREAKFAST BAKE WITH MEDJOOL DATES, BANANAS & MAPLE SYRUP

Basmati rice, quinoa and chia seeds make a great base mix. I've added chewy dried bananas, but you could substitute your favourite dried fruit or leave them out completely if you're not keen. A handful of nuts wouldn't go amiss either, if you have any to spare.

250 g/scant 1½ cups brown basmati rice
50 g/⅓ cup mixed quinoa
50 g/1¾ oz. chia seeds
1.2 litres/5 cups almond milk
a pinch of salt
1 tsp vanilla bean paste
2–3 tbsp maple syrup
100 g/1½ cups dried banana slices

1–2 tbsp sultanas/golden raisins
6–8 medjool dates, pitted
1 tbsp mixed sunflower and pumpkin seeds
1–2 crisp, juicy eating apples, cored and julienned
maple syrup, to serve

SERVES 4

Preheat the oven to 180°C (350°F) Gas 4. Scatter the rice, quinoa and chia seeds over the base of a sheet pan. Stir in the almond milk, salt and vanilla bean paste. Add the maple syrup, banana slices and sultanas/golden raisins. Chop five of the dates and add to the mixture. Cover with foil and bake for about 30–40 minutes, until the rice is soft and the mixture has thickened. Chop the remaining dates and scatter over the top with the sunflower and pumpkin seeds and the apple julienne. Drizzle with maple syrup and serve.

CINNAMON SPICED BRUSCHETTA
WITH BROWN SUGAR PLUMS

Sticky, cinnamon-spiced plums and crisp, oven-baked bruschetta make a truly exquisite start to the day. A cascade of Greek yogurt or creamy, full-fat natural/plain yogurt lifts it right to the top of the ladder of loveliness, but if you're wanting to make it vegan-friendly, simply opt for coconut oil rather than butter and serve it with a coconut or soy milk yogurt, or even a cashew nut cream.

600 g/21 oz. plums
4 medium slices rye sourdough bread
50 g/3½ tbsp butter or coconut oil
50 g/¼ cup dark or light muscovado sugar
1 tsp ground cinnamon

SERVES 4

Preheat the oven to 200°C (400°F) Gas 6. Cut the plums in half and remove the pits. Arrange the plums, cut side up, along one side of a sheet pan. Spread the bread with about half of the butter (or coconut oil). Dot the remaining butter (or oil) over the plums. Mix the sugar and cinnamon together, sprinkle a little over each of the slices of bread and lay them on the other side of the sheet pan. Scatter the remaining cinnamon sugar over the plums. Bake for about 30 minutes, until the bread is crisp and the plums are beautifully soft. Pile the plums onto the bruschetta and serve warm, with yogurt.

ROASTED APRICOTS
WITH GOATS' CURD PUDDLES AND OAT CLUSTERS

Goats' curd is a glorious thing – smooth and creamy, with a perfect suggestion of lemon. Combine it with juicy summer apricots, a crumbly oat and almond topping, bake until bubbling and you have bliss in a breakfast bowl (unless you're having it for dessert, which happens to work beautifully too).

500 g/18 oz. fresh ripe, but firm apricots
2 tbsp thick honey
30 g/2 tbsp softened butter
45 g/½ cup jumbo oats
30 g/scant ½ cup flaked/slivered almonds
20 g/1 tbsp plus 2 tsp light brown
   muscovado sugar
300 g/10½ oz. goats' curd
2–3 tbsp thick honey, to serve

SERVES 4

Preheat the oven to 180°C (350°F) Gas 4. Cut the apricots in half horizontally, remove the pits and arrange on a large sheet pan. Drizzle the honey over. Rub the butter, oats, flaked/slivered almonds and sugar together until the butter is evenly incorporated. Scatter the mixture over the apricots and roast for about 25 minutes, until the oat clusters are golden. Remove the pan from the oven and spoon little puddles of goats' curd here and there. Bake for a further 8–10 minutes, until the curd is melted and has little golden patches.

Serve straight from the pan and drizzle with more honey, to taste.

BAKED ORCHARD FRUITS
WITH MAPLE PECAN AND COCONUT CRISP

This makes a great autumn brunch dish, or a quick and easy pudding, and is absolutely sublime served with coconut yogurt on either occasion. It's a fabulous fusion of orchard fruits, maple syrup, pecan nuts and crispy coconut and is entirely plant-based and absolutely top notch.

1 kg/35 oz. mixed pears, eating apples
   and plums
zest and juice of 1 orange
2–3 tbsp caster/granulated sugar

for the topping
50 g/1¾ oz. coconut oil
2 tbsp light brown muscovado sugar
85 g/generous 1 cup desiccated/dried
   shredded coconut
100 g/1 cup pecan nuts, chopped
3–4 tbsp maple syrup
extra maple syrup and coconut yogurt,
   to serve

SERVES 4

Preheat the oven to 180°C (350°F) Gas 4. Peel the pears and apples, remove their cores and chop them into small dice. Cut the plums in half, remove the pits and cut them into wedges. Scatter the pears, apples and plums over the base of a large roasting pan. Squeeze over the orange juice and sprinkle with the orange zest and sugar. Cook for about 20 minutes, until the fruit is soft.

In the meantime, for the topping, mix the coconut oil, muscovado sugar, coconut, chopped pecans and maple syrup together in a bowl.

Remove the fruit from the oven and scatter the coconut mixture evenly over the top of it. Return the pan to the oven for a further 10 minutes, until the coconut mixture is golden brown.

Serve hot, with extra maple syrup and coconut yogurt.

CHERRY TOMATO, ROASTED PEPPER & SPINACH BOMBAY EGGS

When it comes to choosing my favourite cooked brunch dish, this lovely tomato-rich bake comes tops. It's a winner for a satisfying lunch or supper too.

for the chilli/chile oil
100 ml/^{1}/$_3$ cup plus 1 tbsp extra
    virgin olive oil
1 tbsp dried chilli/red pepper
    flakes

for the Bombay eggs
2 red onions, cut into wedges
1 red (bell) pepper, deseeded
    and cut into strips
1 yellow and 1 orange (bell)
    pepper, deseeded and
    cut into strips
3 tbsp olive oil
2 tsp ground coriander
2 tsp ground cumin
1 tsp ground turmeric
500 g/18 oz. cherry tomatoes

600 ml/2^1/$_2$ cups passata/
    strained tomatoes
50 g/1^3/$_4$ oz. fresh ginger root,
    peeled and finely grated
1 tbsp caster/granulated sugar
1 tsp chilli/red pepper flakes
2–3 big handfuls of fresh baby
    spinach leaves
large bunch of fresh coriander/
    cilantro, coarsely chopped
4 large eggs
150 ml/^{2}/$_3$ cup Greek or full-fat
    natural/plain yogurt
2 tsp nigella seeds (optional)
sea salt and freshly ground
    black pepper

SERVES 4

Combine the oil and chilli/red pepper flakes together in a screw-top jar. Set aside. Preheat the oven to 180°C (350°F) Gas 4. Scatter the onions and (bell) peppers over the base of a large roasting pan and drizzle with the oil. Cook for 20 minutes, until the vegetables have started to soften. Stir in the ground coriander, cumin and turmeric. Return the pan to the oven and cook for a further 10 minutes.

In the meantime, place the cherry tomatoes into a large bowl and pour in the passata. Stir in the grated ginger, sugar and chilli/red pepper flakes. Season with salt and freshly ground black pepper.

Remove the roasting pan from the oven and stir the tomato mix into the (bell) peppers. Return everything to the oven and bake for a further 30 minutes. Stir in the spinach leaves and half of the coriander/cilantro. Make four shallow indentations in the mixture and crack an egg into each. Return to the oven and cook for a further 5–7 minutes, until the eggs are just set. Remove from the oven and drizzle the yogurt over. Scatter over the remaining coriander/cilantro, add a sprinkling of nigella seeds, and then drizzle with the chilli/chile oil. Serve with bread.

LEEK, RED PEPPER & BRIE STRATA

This is lovely with all sorts of different cheeses in place of the brie – punchier washed rind cheeses such as taleggio or zippy goats' cheeses work well, even a strong Cheddar – and feta is fabulous too.

2 fairly large leeks, trimmed and sliced
3 red (bell) peppers, deseeded and cut into strips
3 tbsp olive oil
300 g/10^1/$_2$ oz. (day old, if possible)
    crusty baguette
30 g/2 tbsp butter
600 ml/2^1/$_2$ cups full-fat milk
6 eggs
2 tbsp grain mustard
large handful of freshly chopped mixed herbs
    (tarragon, chives, parsley and dill are fab)
200 g/7 oz. brie, cut into bite-sized cubes

SERVES 4

Preheat the oven to 190°C (375°F) Gas 5. Scatter the leeks and (bell) peppers over the base of a large, deep, lightly greased sheet pan. Drizzle the oil over, and bake in the oven for about 15 minutes, until the vegetables are softened and beginning to char.

In the meantime, cut the baguette into slices and butter them on one side. Cut them in half. Whisk the milk and eggs together in a large bowl. Stir in the grain mustard and about two-thirds of the chopped herbs. Add the bread and the brie to the egg mix and stir everything together. Transfer the mixture to the sheet pan and stir to incorporate the roasted vegetables. Bake for about 40 minutes, until the strata is golden and crisp. Leave to stand for 5 minutes or so. Scatter with the remaining herbs and serve warm.

PORTABELLINI MUSHROOMS WITH SPINACH, CANNELLINI BEANS & LEMON TAHINI DRESSING

Portabellini mushrooms have a really lovely, deliciously savoury flavour and are well worth seeking out, but at a pinch, you could use brown chestnut mushrooms as an alternative if you can't get hold of them.

500 g/18 oz. portabellini
  mushrooms, stalks removed
100 ml/⅓ cup plus 1 tbsp extra
  virgin olive oil
2 garlic cloves, finely chopped
1 tsp fresh thyme leaves
4 generous handfuls of fresh
  baby spinach leaves
400-g/14-oz. can cannellini
  beans, drained and rinsed

for the lemon tahini dressing
75 g/⅓ cup tahini paste
zest and juice of 1 lemon
2 garlic cloves, grated
60–75 ml/¼–⅓ cup water

SERVES 3-4

Preheat the oven to 180°C (350°F) Gas 4. Put the mushrooms on a sheet pan. Mix the oil, garlic and thyme together and spoon all but a tablespoon over the mushrooms. Bake for 10–15 minutes, until the mushrooms are cooked. Stir the spinach and beans together with the remaining spoonful of garlic and thyme oil, and spoon this around the cooked mushrooms. Return everything to the oven for 4–5 minutes, until the spinach is lightly wilted and the beans are warm. Arrange everything on a serving platter and pour over any juices that are left in the pan. Mix all the ingredients for the tahini dressing together in a bowl and drizzle over the mushrooms to serve.

SAVOURY PORRIDGE WITH GREENS & DUKKAH

If you're currently a savoury porridge sceptic, you might well be tempted to turn the page on this one – but savoury porridge is actually quite delicious. It works especially well using spelt porridge flakes rather than traditional oats.

for the dukkah
80 g/generous ½ cup
  sesame seeds
25 g/5 tbsp coriander seeds
20 g/¾ oz. hazelnuts
15 g/½ oz. ground cumin
cracked black pepper

for the porridge
2 large leeks, trimmed and
  coarsely chopped
3 tbsp olive oil
200 g/2 cups spelt porridge
  flakes
1 litre/1 quart good-quality
  vegetable stock

3 tbsp mixed ground seeds
  (optional)
2 large handfuls of baby
  spinach leaves

a large handful of chopped
  kale leaves

for the milled seed mixture
50 g/1¾ oz. sunflower seeds
30 g/¼ cup golden linseeds
20 g/¾ oz. pumpkin seeds

SERVES 4

Preheat the oven to 190°C (375°F) Gas 5. Toss all the ingredients for the dukkah into a sheet pan and bake for about 5 minutes, until the seeds and nuts are lightly toasted. Remove from the oven and crush lightly using a pestle and mortar or pulse briefly in a food processor. Take care not to over-blitz them – the mixture should be coarse and crunchy rather than powder-like. Scatter the leeks over the base of a deep sheet pan. Drizzle with the oil and roast for 10 minutes, until the leeks are starting to colour and soften. Remove the pan from the oven and add the spelt porridge flakes and stock. Stir well, cover with foil, and return the pan to the oven for a further 20 minutes. Stir in the milled seeds (if you are using them) and the greens. Return the pan to the oven for another 5 minutes, until the greens are wilted. Once out of the oven, add a scattering of the dukkah, and serve.

MILLED SEED MIXTURE Add all the seeds to a food processor or nut grinder and blitz until you have a finely textured powder. Store in an airtight jar.

CRUSHED BUTTER BEANS
WITH ROASTED TOMATOES & AVOCADO

This dish is fabulous with crusty bread or sourdough toast for scooping up, and far better than any beans on toast you've ever tasted! I think it makes a perfect brunch dish, and an easy way to feed friends or family when you fancy something hot and tasty. It's a favourite of mine for lunch too.

600 g/21 oz. cherry tomatoes
4 tbsp olive oil
3–4 leeks, trimmed and sliced
1 garlic clove, finely chopped
1 x 400-g/14-oz. can butter/lima beans, drained and rinsed
a bunch of parsley, coarsely chopped
2 ripe, but firm avocados
chilli/chile oil from page 25 (optional)
paprika, to sprinkle
parsley leaves, to garnish

SERVES 4

Preheat the oven to 180°C (350°F) Gas 4. Scatter the cherry tomatoes over a large sheet pan and drizzle the olive oil over. Add the leeks and garlic and toss everything together. Roast for 20 minutes. Remove the sheet pan from the oven and scatter the butter/lima beans evenly over the tomatoes. Crush the beans lightly using the tines of a fork. Scatter over the chopped parsley. Return to the oven for a further 5 minutes.

Remove from the oven. Cut the avocados in half, remove the pits and scoop out the flesh using a teaspoon. Arranged evenly over the beans and tomatoes. Drizzle with chilli/chile oil (if using), add a light sprinkling of paprika and garnish with parsley leaves.

TURMERIC TOFU & ROASTED VEGGIE SCRAMBLE

Roasted vegetables and scrambled tofu make an incredibly pleasing partnership. Here's another one you'll want to get the gloves out for – yellow stained hands aren't a particularly fetching look, and fresh turmeric does tend to leave its mark that way.

1 onion, chopped
1 red (bell) pepper, deseeded and diced
1 orange (bell) pepper, deseeded and diced
200 g/7 oz. cherry tomatoes, halved
100 g/3½ oz. chestnut mushrooms
6 tbsp olive oil
250 g/9 oz. firm tofu
20 g/¾ oz. fresh turmeric, peeled and finely grated
1 tbsp dark soy sauce
a bunch of freshly chopped parsley
sea salt and freshly ground black pepper
chilli/chile oil (see page 25), to serve

SERVES 4

Preheat the oven to 190°C (375°F) Gas 5. Scatter the onion over a large, flat sheet pan. Scatter the (bell) peppers over the onion. Cut the tomatoes in half and scatter these over the onion and (bell) peppers. Slice the mushrooms and add them to the pan. Drizzle with all but 1 tablespoon of the olive oil and roast for about 10 minutes until the vegetables are soft and lightly charred.

Mash the tofu in a large bowl with the remaining tablespoon of oil, the turmeric and soy sauce. Season with salt and pepper and add to the roasted vegetables and stir to combine. Return to the oven for 5 minutes, until everything is hot. Scatter with chopped parsley, and serve with chilli/chile oil.

SMOKY SOY-GLAZED AUBERGINE, LETTUCE & TOMATO PANINI WITH SRIRACHA MAYONNAISE

50 ml/3$\frac{1}{2}$ tbsp date syrup
50 ml/3$\frac{1}{2}$ tbsp dark soy sauce
2 tsp chipotle paste
2 tsp liquid smoke
1 garlic clove, grated
1 medium aubergine/eggplant
1 tsp paprika
4 seeded panini or small ciabatta rolls
2 handfuls of shredded iceberg lettuce
4 ripe but firm tomatoes, sliced
sea salt flakes

for the sriracha mayonnaise
1 quantity (no egg) mayo (see page 86)
2 tbsp sriracha sauce (or to taste)

SERVES 4

When I first made this recipe, it was my original intention to use maple syrup in the glaze. Then I found out mid mise-en-place that my youngest son had polished the last of it off in a pancake-fest. Rather than drop everything, switch the oven off and pop to the shop, I used date syrup – and it made a cracking substitute, I think.

Preheat the oven to 190°C (375°F) Gas 5. Mix the date syrup, soy sauce, chipotle paste, liquid smoke and grated garlic together in a large bowl. Cut off the stalk of the aubergine/eggplant and slice it thinly from the cut end to the base. Dip the aubergine/eggplant slices into the soy mixture, and lay on a prepared sheet pan. Sprinkle with a little paprika and a light sprinkling of salt flakes and bake for about 15–20 minutes, until the slices have a lovely dark copper colour.

Mix the (no egg) mayo and sriracha sauce together.

Cut the bread rolls in half, spread the bases generously with sriracha mayonnaise and pile with lettuce and sliced tomatoes. Top each with several slices of aubergine/eggplant, complete the sandwiches and eat.

SWEET POTATO, CANNELLINI BEAN & KALE FRITTATA

2 red onions, sliced from root to tip
1 large sweet potato, peeled and diced
4 tbsp olive oil
1 x 400-g/14-oz. can cannellini beans
150 g/scant 1$\frac{1}{2}$ cups Cheddar cheese, grated
2-3 big handfuls of kale, trimmed and
　coarsely chopped
8 eggs
sea salt and freshly ground black pepper
chilli/chile oil, to serve (optional)

SERVES 4

There's something very satisfying about this combination. The bonus is that some of the kale is left poking out of the egg mixture and when it cooks, it crisps up – so there's a soft cheesy-creaminess with the base and then a light crunch on the top.

Preheat the oven to 190°C (375°F) Gas 5. Scatter the onions in the base of a lightly greased and lined deep sheet pan. Scatter the sweet potatoes evenly over the onions. Drizzle with the oil, season, and roast for about 25 minutes, until the potato and onions are cooked and just starting to char slightly.

Drain and rinse the cannellini beans. Remove the sheet pan from the oven and scatter the beans evenly into the pan. Sprinkle the grated cheese over and scatter over the chopped kale.

Beat the eggs until smooth, season them, and then pour them evenly over everything in the sheet pan. Return the pan to the oven and bake for about 15–20 minutes more, until the eggs have set.

Serve hot, drizzled with chilli/chile oil (if desired).

VEG BOX HEROES

ROAST BUTTERNUT SQUASH WITH BLACK BELUGA
LENTILS, POMEGRANATES & PINE NUTS

2 small butternut squash, halved
   and deseeded
4–5 tbsp olive oil
a handful of fresh thyme leaves
2 tbsp freshly chopped rosemary
2 large leeks, trimmed and chopped
300 g/10½ oz. baby plum tomatoes
1 x 400-g/14-oz. can black beluga lentils
sea salt flakes and freshly ground
   black pepper

for the dressing
50 ml/3½ tbsp olive oil
50 ml/3½ tbsp pomegranate molasses

to serve
50 g/scant ½ cup toasted pine nuts
3–4 tbsp pomegranate seeds
rocket/arugula leaves

SERVES 4

Roasting the squash in its skin gives the whole vegetable such a fabulous texture and the skin is unbelievably good to eat. Serve with a rocket/arugula salad.

Preheat the oven to 190°C (375°F) Gas 5. Lightly score a diamond pattern into the flesh of the squash using the tip of a sharp knife. Drizzle with a little of the oil, sprinkle with the thyme and rosemary, place on a flat sheet pan and bake for 15 minutes. Remove the sheet pan from the oven and push the squash over to one side. Scatter the chopped leeks and whole baby plum tomatoes on the other side of the pan and drizzle with the remaining oil. Scatter with salt flakes and freshly ground black pepper and return to the oven for another 20 minutes, until the flesh of the squash is soft and the leeks and tomatoes are lightly charred. Scoop the leeks and tomatoes into a large bowl. Drain and rinse the lentils, and add them to the bowl. Mix the olive oil and pomegranate molasses together for the dressing and add about half to the lentil mixture. Pile the mixture into the squash hollows and return the sheet pan to the oven. Bake for 5 minutes, until the lentil filling is just heated through.

Remove from the oven, drizzle over the remaining dressing, scatter with pine nuts and pomegranate seeds and add a good grinding of black pepper.

ROOT VEGETABLE & PEAR SHEET PAN CRISP

1.5 kg/3 lb. 5 oz. mixed root vegetables
   (carrots, parsnips, squash,
   beetroots/beets etc.), diced
1 large leek, trimmed and thinly sliced
2 red onions, cut into wedges
4 tomatoes, roughly chopped
4 tbsp olive oil
3 ripe, but firm pears, cored and diced
2 tbsp brown rice syrup
3 tbsp grain mustard

for the topping
200 g/2 cups spelt flakes
100 ml/⅓ cup plus 1 tbsp olive oil
50 g/½ cup ground almonds
20 g/⅓ cup nutritional yeast flakes
2 tbsp finely chopped chives
rocket/arugula leaves, olive oil and balsamic
   vinegar, to serve

SERVES 4-6

I was looking for something a little different to do with a box of spelt flakes and I was rather pleased with the light, crisp topping it created. I've used olive oil as the fat, and nutritional yeast flakes that add a nutty, cheesy flavour but mean that it is still entirely plant-based.

Preheat the oven to 190°C (375°F) Gas 5. Peel the root vegetables and cut them into large, even dice. Scatter the root vegetables over a roasting pan. Add the leek slices, onion wedges and the chopped tomatoes to the pan. Drizzle the olive oil over the vegetables and toss everything together until evenly coated. Roast for about 35 minutes, until the vegetables are almost soft. Remove the pan from the oven and add the pears. Drizzle the brown rice syrup over everything, add the grain mustard and toss everything together so that all the vegetables are coated with mustard. Roast for a further 10 minutes. For the topping, combine the spelt flakes, olive oil, almonds and nutritional yeast flakes. Scatter the topping over the bake and return to the oven for a further 15 minutes, until the topping is crisp and golden.

Sprinkle with the chives and serve with a rocket/arugula salad, dressed with olive oil and balsamic vinegar.

PURPLE SPROUTING BROCCOLI & FLAGEOLET BEANS WITH PRESERVED LEMON MAYO

This easy-peasy combo of crispy, lightly charred broccoli, soft garlicky beans, crunchy lemony crumbs and zippy, unctuous preserved lemon mayo makes a fabulous light lunch.

for the mayo
1 egg
1 garlic clove, grated
1 tbsp Dijon mustard
juice of 1/2 lemon
250 ml/1 cup plus 1 tbsp sunflower oil
1/4–1/2 preserved lemon

350 g/12 oz. purple sprouting broccoli
1 x 400-g/14-oz. can flageolet beans
3 tbsp olive oil
2 garlic cloves, finely chopped
a large handful of fresh parsley,
   finely chopped
3 tbsp panko crumbs
zest of 1 lemon

SERVES 4

To make the preserved lemon mayonnaise, put the egg, grated garlic, Dijon mustard and lemon juice into a jug/pitcher. Whiz everything together using a stick blender. Slowly add the oil, keeping the blender going and pouring in a steady stream, until all the oil is incorporated and the mixture is thick and light.

Rinse the salt from the preserved lemon, remove the inner flesh and discard. Finely chop the softened skin and add it to the mayonnaise. Cover and refrigerate until ready to use.

Preheat the oven to 180°C (350°F) Gas 4. Trim the broccoli. Leave the stalks quite long, but peel away any tough bits using a vegetable peeler. Lay the broccoli over a sheet pan and cook for 10–15 minutes, until the broccoli is al dente, but starting to crisp on the florets. Drain and rinse the beans. Pop them into a bowl and add the oil, chopped garlic and parsley. Remove the broccoli from the oven and spoon the beans over. Mix the panko crumbs and lemon zest together and scatter this over the top. Return the sheet pan to the oven and cook for a further 5 minutes, until the beans are warmed through. Take care not to leave the pan in for too long, or the beans will dry and crack – they just need to be warm rather than super-hot. Serve with the preserved lemon mayo.

ROASTED RED CABBAGE
WITH CHARRED BROCCOLI, CHERRIES & ALMONDS

1 red cabbage
4 tbsp olive oil
600 g/21 oz. broccoli
50 g/1/2 cup toasted, flaked/slivered almonds
100 g/3/4 cup dried cherries
a bunch of spring onions/scallions, chopped
a large bunch of fresh dill, coarsely chopped
sea salt and freshly ground black pepper

for the balsamic dressing
40 ml/3 tbsp extra virgin olive oil
30 ml/2 tbsp balsamic vinegar
1 tsp caster/granulated sugar
sea salt flakes
roasted chilli jam (see page 121), to serve

SERVES 4

Red cabbage and broccoli roast beautifully and have an awesome affinity with sweet, tangy balsamic vinegar dressing. I've added plump juicy dried cherries and flaky almonds for more flavour and crunch, and I like to serve this with chilli jam.

Preheat the oven to 200°C (400°F) Gas 6. Cut the red cabbage into wedges and arrange them over a sheet pan. Drizzle with the oil, season and roast for 10 minutes. Chop the broccoli very finely – to an almost rice-like texture – and scatter it around the wedges of cabbage. Sprinkle with flaked/slivered almonds, return the pan to the oven, and cook for a further 10 minutes.

Mix all the ingredients for the dressing together and season with salt flakes.

Remove the pan from the oven and gently push the cooked almonds into the broccoli using a fork. Drizzle everything with the dressing and scatter with the dried cherries, chopped spring onions/scallions and dill. Serve with chilli jam.

ROASTED HERITAGE BEETROOTS WITH MUSHROOMS, RED ONIONS, LENTILS, BEETROOT & ROSEMARY CRISPS & BALSAMIC DRESSING

My youngest son loves this – he likes to scatter it with bite-sized chunks of salty feta – which works really well. Nuggets of zesty goats' cheese work too. As it is here – minus cheese, it's still a pretty special dish for anyone following a plant-based diet.

1 kg/35 oz. mixed heritage
    beetroots/beets
3 red onions, cut into wedges
250 g/3$\frac{1}{2}$ cups chestnut mushrooms,
    sliced
3 tbsp olive oil
5–6 sprigs freshly chopped rosemary
1 x 400-g/14-oz. can green lentils
6 tbsp olive oil
3 tbsp balsamic vinegar
1 tsp caster/granulated sugar
1 garlic clove, finely grated
freshly chopped mixed herbs
    (dill, chives, parsley), to serve

SERVES 4

Preheat the oven to 190°C (375°F) Gas 5. Peel the beetroots/beets and cut them into wedges. Arrange them over the base of a sheet pan. Add the onions to the pan and scatter the mushrooms evenly over the top. Drizzle with olive oil and scatter over the chopped rosemary. Roast for about 45–50 minutes, until the beetroots/beets are soft.

Drain and rinse the lentils and spoon them onto the sheet pan. Return the pan to the oven for 5 minutes, until the lentils are heated through.

Mix the olive oil, balsamic vinegar, sugar and garlic together.

Remove the pan from the oven, drizzle over the dressing, scatter over the freshly chopped herbs and serve warm, or at room temperature.

CHARRED HISPI CABBAGE
WITH DRIED CHERRY & JUNIPER BUTTER & CRISPY FREEKEH

for the butter
100 g/½ cup minus 1 tbsp salted butter,
    softened
20 juniper berries
1 generous tsp freshly chopped rosemary
50 g/1¾ oz. dried cherries, roughly chopped

1 hispi (pointed) cabbage, trimmed
3–4 tbsp olive oil
250 g/9-oz. pouch pre-cooked freekeh
zest and juice of 1 lemon
sea salt and freshly ground black pepper
freshly chopped parsley, to garnish

SERVES 3–4

When cabbage comes out of the oven, still with a little bite, its sweet flavour intensified against crisp, charred edges, you should prepare yourself for a treat.

Put the butter into a bowl. Crush the juniper berries using a pestle and mortar. Add the juniper, rosemary and dried cherries to the bowl, and work everything together with a fork, until everything is evenly mixed.

Lay a piece of clingfilm/plastic wrap on a clean work surface. Form the butter into a small sausage shape, and roll up in the clingfilm/plastic wrap. Give the package a little roll backwards and forwards to create an even shape and swizzle the ends to seal. Transfer to the fridge to firm up.

Preheat the oven to 190°C (375°F) Gas 5. Cut the cabbage in half from root to tip, and then cut each half into three or four wedges. Arrange them on a sheet pan and drizzle with half of the oil. Bake for 10 minutes. Remove the pan from the oven, scatter over the freekeh and drizzle over the remaining olive oil. Return to the oven and cook for a further 5 minutes or so, until the freekeh is hot and crisp and the edges of the cabbage are lightly charred. Remove from the oven, scatter over the lemon zest and juice, season with salt and black pepper and garnish with freshly chopped parsley. Serve while hot, with thin slices of the juniper and cherry butter melting into the leaves.

ROASTED LEEK & APPLE WITH VINAIGRETTE & KALE

There's a classic French dish called Leeks Vinaigrette, which shows off the wonderful affinity that the allium has with unctuous mustardy sauces. I think roasting brings out an extra depth of flavour.

4–5 leeks, cut into 5-cm/2-inch pieces
5 tbsp olive oil
3 crisp, red-skinned eating apples,
    cored and each cut into 6 wedges
2 tsp caster/granulated sugar
3 handfuls of curly kale
for the vinaigrette
100 ml/⅓ cup plus 1 tbsp olive oil
30 ml/2 tbsp white wine or cider vinegar
20–25 g/¾–1 oz. caster/granulated sugar
20 g/4 tsp Dijon mustard
sea salt and freshly ground black pepper

SERVES 4

Preheat the oven to 190°C (375°F) Gas 5. Arrange the leeks over a sheet pan, drizzle with 2 tablespoons of the oil and roast for 15 minutes. Add the apple wedges to the sheet pan, drizzle with a further 2 tablespoons of the olive oil and sprinkle evenly with the sugar. Roast for a further 15 minutes, until the apples are soft, but still holding their shape.

Remove the tough central stalk from the kale, pop it into a large bowl and toss it with the remaining oil. Scatter the kale over the sheet pan and return to the oven for 5 minutes, until the kale is crisp.

In the meantime, whisk all the ingredients for the vinaigrette together until emulsified.

Serve the leeks warm, spooning over the dressing just before serving.

ROASTED PIRI-PIRI SPROUTS, LEEK RIBBONS, CHESTNUTS, DRIED CRANBERRIES & REBLOCHON

Piri-piri's perky and piquant citrus notes add a special something to ever-so-slightly-crisp sprouts, which sweeten and mellow as they cook. When you add them to crunchy chestnuts, chewy dried cranberries, pools of melting cheese and fruity cranberry sauce, you have a combination that is impossible to resist. To ring the changes, substitute any soft, washed rind cheese – I particularly like Taleggio and Camembert.

500 g/5 cups Brussels sprouts, halved
3 tbsp olive oil
2 tsp piri-piri spice mix
4 leeks, trimmed and cut into
   5-cm/2-inch pieces
180–200 g/6¼–7 oz. ready-to-use chestnuts
300 g/10½ oz. Reblochon cheese
50 g/⅓ cup dried cranberries
1 tbsp finely chopped fresh rosemary
3 tbsp cranberry sauce
fresh rosemary sprigs, to garnish

SERVES 4

Preheat the oven to 190°C (375°F) Gas 5. Put the Brussels sprouts into a roasting pan. Drizzle over the oil, add the piri-piri spice mix and toss well until the sprouts are evenly coated. Roast for about 10 minutes, until the sprouts are starting to brown lightly, but are still slightly crunchy.

Scatter the leeks over the sprouts and cook for another 10 minutes, until everything is nice and golden. Remove the pan from the oven, scatter over the chestnuts and dot with nuggets of Reblochon. Sprinkle over the dried cranberries and the chopped rosemary and return the pan to the oven.

Cook for a further 5–8 minutes or so, until the cheese is just melting. Transfer to a warm serving platter, add a small spoonful of cranberry sauce here and there and garnish with sprigs of rosemary.

SLOW-BAKED ONIONS WITH GOATS' CHEESE, CRISPY BAGUETTE CROUTONS, WALNUTS & BALSAMIC DRESSING

450 g/1 lb. small red onions,
    halved from root to tip
1 tsp fresh thyme leaves
1 tbsp freshly chopped rosemary
2 tsp caster/granulated sugar
4 tbsp olive oil
1 small baguette
250 g/9 oz. goats' cheese
3 tbsp walnut pieces
sea salt and freshly ground black pepper

for the dressing
60 ml/¼ cup olive oil
60 ml/¼ cup balsamic vinegar
30 ml/2 tbsp date syrup
fresh basil leaves, to garnish

SERVES 4

This comforting combination of meltingly soft onions, oozy cheese and crunchy bites of baguette is absolutely top notch. Red onions have a lovely mild flavour when roasted. A rocket/arugula salad is lovely with this.

Preheat the oven to 190°C (375°F) Gas 5. Arrange the onion halves over the central area of a large sheet pan. Scatter with the thyme leaves, chopped rosemary and sugar. Season with salt and freshly ground black pepper, drizzle with half of the oil and roast for about 20 minutes, until the onions are starting to soften. Cut the crusts off the baguette (probably nibble on some), and tear the bread into funky-shaped pieces. Toss them with the remaining olive oil and arrange around the edges of the pan. Bake for about 10–15 minutes, until crisp and golden (the onions should still be cooking nicely in the centre). Remove the croutons from the pan and set aside.

Break the goats' cheese up into bite-sized nuggets and scatter over the onions. Toss the walnuts over the top and return to the oven for 5–8 minutes, until the cheese is melting. Spoon the mixture onto a pretty serving plate.

To make the dressing, mix the oil, balsamic vinegar and date syrup together, and season to taste with salt and freshly ground black pepper. Drizzle the dressing over the onions and cheese, scatter with the crispy baguette croutons and garnish with fresh basil leaves. Serve warm.

SPICED AUBERGINE, GARLIC & TOMATO SOUP

1 red onion, roughly chopped
1 small aubergine/eggplant, cut into chunks
2 garlic cloves, finely chopped
6 large ripe tomatoes, chopped
1 tbsp Berbere spice mix (see page 82)
3 tbsp olive oil
600 ml/2½ cups passata/strained tomatoes
600 ml/2½ cups vegetable stock
2 tbsp good-quality tomato ketchup
1–2 tbsp finely chopped parsley
2–3 tbsp olive oil
smoked paprika, to serve

SERVES 4

Roasted vegetables make great soup – and there's absolutely no point in roasting the veg and then doing everything else on the stovetop, when it can all go in the oven and save on washing up. A stick blender is handy here, but if you don't have one, then you can simply transfer everything to a liquidizer. This is one where good-quality tomato ketchup adds a little necessary sweetness to the mix.

Preheat the oven to 180°C (350°F) Gas 4. Scatter the chopped onion over the base of a roasting pan. Add the chopped aubergine/eggplant to the pan with the garlic. Add the chopped tomatoes to the pan with the spice mix and olive oil. Give everything a good stir and cook for 15–20 minutes. Pour in the passata/strained tomatoes and vegetable stock. Return the pan to the oven and cook for a further 15–20 minutes. Blitz until smooth using a stick blender or liquidizer. Stir in the parsley. Drizzle with olive oil, sprinkle with smoked paprika and serve hot.

ROASTED PARSNIPS, LEEKS, CAULIFLOWER, CABBAGE & FENNEL WITH GREEN LENTILS

400 g/14 oz. parsnips, peeled and
    cut into batons
1 medium fennel bulb, cut into wedges
5–6 tbsp olive oil
3 tbsp brown rice syrup or maple syrup
1 medium cauliflower, broken into florets
2 small leeks, trimmed and sliced
1 small pointy cabbage, thickly sliced
1 tsp fennel seeds
1 x 400-g/14-oz. can green lentils
sea salt and freshly ground black pepper
dill or fennel fronds, to garnish

for the dressing
100 ml/$\frac{1}{3}$ cup plus 1 tbsp extra virgin
    olive oil
25 g/1 oz. grain mustard
30 ml/2 tbsp cider vinegar
15 g/$\frac{1}{2}$ oz. caster/granulated sugar
zest of 1 lemon

SERVES 4

This medley really qualifies as roasted veggie heaven – the heat of the oven brings out the natural sweetness of each vegetable and creates the most delicious result.

Preheat the oven to 190°C (375°F) Gas 5. Put the parsnip batons and fennel wedges into a large bowl and add half of the oil and the brown rice syrup or maple syrup. Toss to coat everything, and then arrange on a sheet pan. Roast for about 15 minutes, until the vegetables are beginning to soften. Arrange the cauliflower florets over the sheet pan. Scatter the leeks evenly over the pan. Cut the cabbage slices into halves or quarters, and lay them here and there over the pan. Drizzle over the remaining oil, sprinkle with fennel seeds, and season. Return the sheet pan to the oven and roast for a further 20 minutes or so – until the vegetables are soft and slightly charred on the edges.

Drain the lentils and rinse them under the cold water tap. When the vegetables are cooked, spoon the lentils randomly but evenly over the vegetables and return the pan to the oven for 5 minutes, until the lentils are just warmed through.

Meanwhile, whisk all the ingredients for the dressing together in a bowl. Remove the sheet pan from the oven, drizzle the dressing over the vegetables and garnish with dill or fennel fronds.

PARSNIPS MOLLY PARKIN

This dish was originally developed by a friend of the Welsh journalist and top parsnip hater Molly Parkin, in order to convince her they were a vegetable more than worthy of her affection. He fried them in a pan and layered them in a dish with sliced tomatoes, cheese and cream and she did, in fact, change her mind.

750 g/26 oz. parsnips
4 tbsp olive oil
1 leek
400 g/14 oz. cherry tomatoes, halved
400 ml/1$\frac{3}{4}$ cups double/heavy cream
200 g/2$\frac{1}{4}$ cups strong cheese, such as
    Mature Cheddar or Gruyère, grated
50 g/1 cup panko crumbs
sea salt flakes and freshly ground
    black pepper
green salad, to serve

SERVES 4

Preheat the oven to 190°C (375°F) Gas 5. Peel the parsnips and cut them into slices. Arrange them over a deep sheet pan and drizzle with the olive oil. Roast for about 20 minutes, until they are light golden and just starting to soften. Wash and trim the leek and cut it into slices. Add it to the sheet pan and roast for a further 10 minutes.

Carefully mix the cherry tomatoes into the roasted vegetables. Mix the cream and all but a small handful of the cheese together. Season with salt flakes and freshly ground black pepper. Pour the mixture over the vegetables, and then scatter the remaining cheese and the panko crumbs over the top. Bake for a further 10–15 minutes, until everything is bubbling hot and the crumbs are golden. Serve with a green salad.

PAN HAGGERTY

This is a traditional stovetop-one-pan-potato-dish that comes from the north of England, and very tasty it is too. Here, I've given it the sheet pan treatment, and I think it's fab. You might want to line the sheet pan with baking parchment or a silicone mat because the crispy bits around the edges do tend to stick.

1 kg/35 oz. floury potatoes,
  peeled and thinly sliced
3 brown or white onions, thinly sliced
3–4 tbsp olive oil
250 g/2³/₄ cups extra mature Cheddar
  cheese, grated
a small handful of fresh thyme leaves
mixed salad, to serve

SERVES 4

Preheat the oven to 190°C (375°F) Gas 5. Put the sliced potatoes and onions into a bowl. Pour in the olive oil and add all but a handful of the cheese. Add the thyme leaves and toss everything together so that the onions and the cheese are evenly distributed. Spread the mixture evenly over a greased or lined sheet pan and cover with foil. Bake for about 50 minutes, and then remove the foil and scatter over the remaining cheese. Bake for a further 10 minutes or so, until the cheese is melted and golden.

Serve hot, with a mixed salad.

ROSEMARY & THYME ANNA POTATOES

In my work as a professional private chef, I often serve Anna potatoes - they seem to be universally loved. Of course then, I make sure to painstakingly arrange the potatoes in concentric-slightly-overlapping layers. At home, I just freestyle – as long as they're level in the pan to make sure that they cook evenly, I think a more relaxed presentation is quite nice – but feel free to be more precise if you're cooking them with a special meal in mind.

1 kg/35 oz. floury potatoes,
  peeled and very thinly sliced
150 g/²/₃ cup melted butter
1 tbsp fresh thyme leaves
2 tbsp freshly chopped rosemary
sea salt and freshly ground black pepper
a 30 x 17 x 2.5 cm/11³/₄ x 6³/₄ x 1 inch
  brownie pan, lightly greased and
  lined with baking parchment

SERVES 4-6

Preheat the oven to 200°C (400°F) Gas 6. Don't wash the potato slices, as the starch in them will help them stick together – simply put them into a large bowl and pour in the melted butter (I melt the butter in the oven, but a microwave will do, if you prefer). Add the herbs and season with salt and freshly ground black pepper, then give everything a really good stir, so that the butter and herbs thoroughly coat the potato slices. Spread the potatoes in the prepared brownie pan, cover with foil and bake for about 50 minutes–1 hour – removing the foil halfway through the cooking time – until the potatoes are soft and golden on the top. Serve immediately.

MEDITERRANEAN MAGIC

SPRING VEGETABLES BARIGOULE WITH GREMOLATA

Just-cooked baby spring vegetables grow together and go together to create such a stunning dish and the zingy-fresh gremolata topping makes it super-special. Please take care not to overcook the vegetables though, because the pleasure is in the bright, vibrant flavours and colours, and it doesn't take too long to overcook them and lose both.

for the vegetables
juice of 1 large lemon
   (use the zest for the gremolata)
2 globe artichokes
2 medium fennel bulbs
3 tbsp olive oil
250 ml/1 cup plus 1 tbsp white wine
1.25 litres/5 cups good-quality
   vegetable stock
1 fresh bay leaf
a few tarragon sprigs
300 g/10½ oz. baby carrots
250 g/9 oz. radishes
250 g/generous 1½ cups fresh peas
450 g/1 lb. asparagus, trimmed
125 g/4½ oz. tenderstem broccoli/broccolini
   or purple sprouting broccoli, trimmed

for the dressing
4 tbsp brown rice syrup
4 tbsp extra virgin olive oil
juice of 1 lemon
   (use the zest for the gremolata)

for the gremolata
finely grated zest of 2 lemons
a bunch of parsley, freshly chopped
1 garlic clove, finely chopped

SERVES 4

For the vegetables, preheat the oven to 200°C (400°F) Gas 6. Fill a bowl with cold water and add the lemon juice. Snap off the woody outside leaves of the artichokes and cut off the stems and tough tops. Cut them in half and remove the fluffy centres with a teaspoon. Cut each half into three and plunge them immediately into the acidulated water, to stop them from turning brown.

Trim the fennel bulbs, and cut them into wedges. Arrange them on a large, deep sheet pan and drizzle with the oil. Cook for 15 minutes, until they are starting to turn golden. Remove the sheet pan from the oven and pour in the white wine and stock. Add the bay leaf and tarragon sprigs. Add the baby carrots and radishes to the pan. Take a piece of baking parchment and lay it over the liquid (much like you would use a cartouche if you were cooking on the hob/stovetop) and cook for about 10 minutes, until the carrots are just starting to soften.

Remove the sheet pan from the oven, take away the cartouche and add the fresh peas, asparagus and broccoli stems. Cover with the parchment and return to the oven for a further 5 minutes, until the vegetables are just cooked and still have their lovely bright colour. Immediately drain away the stock, and reserve it for something else.

In the meantime, whisk all the ingredients for the dressing together in a bowl.

For the gremolata, the lemon zest, chopped parsley and garlic together in a separate bowl.

Serve the vegetables warm, drizzled with the dressing and scattered with the gremolata.

POTATO & ROSEMARY PIZZA

This pizza is vegan-friendly, made from the kind of staples you generally have in the house – and if you use fast-action yeast, it's doesn't take too long from start to finish either. Simplicity at its winning best. If possible, cut and soak the potato slices in cold water for 30 minutes or so before making the pizza bases. This helps the potatoes crisp more efficiently.

for the pizza base
500 g/3½–3⅔ cups strong plain bread flour
1 tsp fine sea salt
1 tsp caster/granulated sugar
7 g/¼ oz. sachet fast-action dried yeast
1 tbsp olive oil
about 300 ml/1¼ cups hand-hot water

for the topping
600 g/21 oz. smallish floury potatoes, soaked
    and very thinly sliced (as intro)
4 tbsp olive oil
2 tbsp finely chopped rosemary
a large bunch of spring onions/scallions,
    chopped
sea salt and freshly ground black pepper

SERVES 4

Preheat the oven to 200°C (400°F) Gas 6. Put the flour into a large bowl and stir in the salt and sugar. Add the yeast and mix well. Pour in the olive oil, and add enough hand-hot water to bring the mixture together into a soft, but not sticky dough. Knead the dough for 5–10 minutes, until smooth. Divide the dough into two and roll each piece into a rectangle to fit the base of two sheet pans.

Drain the water from the potatoes and rinse them under running cold water one final time. Dry thoroughly on paper towels or a clean kitchen towel. Toss them into a large bowl with the olive oil, rosemary and a generous sprinkling of salt flakes and black pepper, until all the slices are evenly coated.

Scatter the spring onions/scallions between the two bases. Top with the potato slices, overlapping the potato edges very slightly, until the bases are covered. Bake the pizzas for about 20 minutes or so, until the potatoes are cooked and crispy golden at the edges. Cut into squares and serve at once.

OVEN-BAKED BUTTERNUT SQUASH, SAFFRON & ROSEMARY RISOTTO

4 g/⅛ oz. saffron filaments
1 onion, chopped
25 g/1½ tbsp butter
2 tbsp olive oil
400 g/14 oz. peeled, deseeded butternut
    squash, cut into bite-sized cubes
300 g/1⅔ cups carnaroli rice
120 ml/½ cup dry white wine
800 ml/generous 3¼ cups well-flavoured
    vegetable stock
1 tbsp freshly chopped rosemary

for the mantecatura
50 g/3½ tbsp butter
80 g/1¼ cups Parmesan cheese, grated

SERVES 4

Having had a house in Italy for 10 years, I do have a soft spot for a good risotto. Purists may tut-tut at the idea of making one in the oven, but it does work surprisingly well – just keep an eye on timing, so that the rice doesn't overcook.

Preheat the oven to 200°C (400°F) Gas 6. Put the saffron filaments into a small bowl and pour on a couple of tablespoons of just-boiled water. Leave to infuse. Scatter the chopped onion over the base of a deep sheet pan. Add the butter and olive oil. Transfer to the oven for 10 minutes, until the onion is starting to soften.

Add the butternut squash to the sheet pan. Stir in the rice, until everything is coated with the oil and butter. Pour in the wine, stock and saffron and stir in the rosemary. Cover the pan with foil and return to the oven. Cook for about 20 minutes or so, until the rice is cooked but still has a little bite. Remove from the oven, stir in the butter and Parmesan for the mantecatura and serve.

ROASTED MEDITERRANEAN VEGETABLES WITH BALSAMIC DRESSING

When I say '1 fairly large courgette/zucchini' here, I don't mean the sort that is on the verge of classification as a small marrow – huge courgettes/zucchinis might look fairly impressive on the outside, but the flesh can become quite lacking in flavour, as the water content rises and the seeds become bigger – often giving the vegetable a slightly bitter taste. Make sure to roast until the vegetables are looking a little charred at the edges here and there – it will take the best part of an hour, but will reward with bags of flavour.

2 red onions, cut into wedges
1 fairly large courgette/zucchini, sliced
1 medium aubergine/eggplant,
    cut into bite-sized chunks
1 red (bell) pepper, deseeded
    and cut into strips
1 yellow (bell) pepper, deseeded
    and cut into strips
1 orange (bell) pepper, deseeded
    and cut into strips
400 g/14 oz. cherry tomatoes
5 tbsp olive oil
a good scattering of fresh thyme leaves
3 tbsp balsamic vinegar
sea salt flakes and freshly ground
    black pepper
fresh basil leaves, to garnish

SERVES 4

Preheat the oven to 190°C (375°F) Gas 5. Scatter the onion wedges over a sheet pan. Scatter the courgette/zucchini, aubergine/eggplant and (bell) peppers over the pan. Leave the tomatoes whole and scatter the tomatoes over. Drizzle everything with the oil, season with salt flakes, freshly ground black pepper and lots of fresh thyme leaves. Cook for 50 minutes–1 hour, turning everything halfway through the cooking time, until the vegetables are shiny and soft, and lightly charred at the edges.

Drizzle over the balsamic vinegar, garnish with fresh basil leaves and serve warm or at room temperature.

FONDANT TOMATOES WITH BASIL & BURRATA

Warm, sweet roasted baby plum tomatoes and fridge-cold creamy burrata make a combination that is out-of-this-world irresistible. Be generous with the extra virgin olive oil, as it will help create the most incredible juices, which marry together with those from the tomatoes and create something magical when they meet with the dreamy burrata.

500 g/18 oz. baby plum tomatoes, halved
300 g/10½ oz. baby plum tomatoes
  on the vine
4–5 tbsp olive oil
2 tsp caster/granulated sugar
2 tsp fresh thyme leaves
400 g/14 oz. (drained weight) burrata
sea salt and freshly ground black pepper
fresh basil leaves, to garnish

SERVES 4

Preheat the oven to 150°C (300°F) Gas 2. Lay the baby plum tomatoes, cut side up, on a large, flat sheet pan. Cut the baby tomatoes on the vine into little clusters of two or three, and arrange them on the sheet pan as well. Drizzle with the oil, sprinkle with sugar and season with salt and freshly ground black pepper. Scatter over the thyme leaves. Cook for about 30 minutes or so – until the tomatoes are meltingly soft and sticky. Remove from the oven and leave to cool slightly. Gently tear the burrata into pieces and arrange it over the tomatoes. Scatter with fresh basil leaves and serve warm with crusty bread for dipping into the juices.

BABY PLUM TOMATO CLAFOUTIS

You may well have come across a cherry clafoutis – the classic French dessert that's not quite a custard, nor an omelette, nor a gratin, but is nevertheless very well loved. This is my savoury version, and it makes a first-rate dish for a light lunch. It's great for a picnic basket too.

8 eggs
120 g/1⅓ cups extra mature Cheddar
  cheese, grated
95 g/⅔ cup plain/all-purpose flour
300 ml/10½ fl. oz. double/heavy cream
300 g/10½ oz. baby plum tomatoes
  (or use cherry tomatoes)
30 g/scant ½ cup Parmesan cheese
sea salt and freshly ground black pepper
fresh basil leaves, to garnish
a 30 x 17 x 2.5 cm/11¾ x 6¾ x 1 inch
  brownie pan, lightly greased and lined
  with baking parchment

SERVES 4-6

Preheat the oven to 190°C (375°F) Gas 5. Beat the eggs well, and then stir in the grated cheese. Slowly add in the flour, whisking until it has been fully incorporated. Stir in the cream. Season the mixture with salt and freshly ground black pepper.

Pour the mixture into the prepared pan and scatter the tomatoes evenly over. Bake for about 20–25 minutes, until the clafoutis has set. Make shavings from the Parmesan using a potato peeler and sprinkle them across the top of the clafoutis. Garnish with fresh basil leaves, cut into squares and serve.

CARROT TART TATIN SQUARES WITH GINGER & MINT YOGURT

1.5 kg/3 lb. 5 oz. carrots
250 g/9 oz. shallots, peeled
3 tbsp honey
2 tbsp olive oil
1 tbsp fresh thyme leaves
30 g/2 tbsp butter, softened
3 tbsp light brown muscovado sugar
300 g/10 1/2 oz. ready-made puff pastry
sea salt and freshly ground black pepper

for the yogurt
200 g/scant 1 cup natural/plain
    full fat yogurt
2 cm/3/4 inch fresh piece of ginger root,
    finely grated
1 garlic clove, grated
a small bunch of mint leaves, roughly torn
extra mint, to garnish

a 30 x 17 x 2.5 cm/11 3/4 x 6 3/4 x 1 inch
    brownie pan

MAKES 12 SQUARES

When you put glossy, caramelized carrots, soft candied shallots and crisp flaky pastry together, you really can't fail to end up with something very special, and this tatin is certainly that.

Preheat the oven to 190°C (375°F) Gas 5. Cut the carrots into triangular chunks about 2 cm/3/4 inch wide at the base. Scatter them over the base of a sheet pan and add the peeled shallots. Mix the honey, olive oil and thyme leaves together and spoon the mixture over the vegetables. Season and roast for about 30 minutes, until the carrots have started to soften. Remove the pan from the oven and stir in the butter and muscovado sugar.

Roll the pastry out to fit the pan and place it carefully over the vegetables, tucking the edges in.

Bake for about 25 minutes or so, until the pastry is golden and crisp. Remove from the oven and leave to settle for 4–5 minutes, before turning out and inverting onto a board and cutting into squares.

Stir the yogurt, grated ginger and grated garlic together in a bowl. Add the torn mint leaves and season with a little salt and freshly ground black pepper. Arrange the carrot tatin squares on a pretty serving dish and garnish with extra mint leaves. Serve the yogurt in a bowl alongside.

ROAST MINI PEPPERS WITH FETA, OLIVES & PESTO

If you want to make this dish plant-based only, substitute a vegan cheese or serve everything without cheese, but add the juice of a lemon to the oil, basil and garlic, replacing the more traditional pesto with a dressing.

400 g/14 oz. mini (bell) peppers,
    halved and deseeded
250 g/9 oz. cherry tomatoes, quartered
2 garlic cloves, finely chopped
4 tbsp olive oil
100 g/1 cup pitted black olives
200 g/7 oz. feta cheese
sea salt and freshly ground black pepper

for the pesto
80 ml/1/3 cup olive oil
2 garlic cloves, chopped
80 g/1 1/4 cups Parmesan cheese, grated
40 g/1/3 cup pine nuts/kernals
2 big handfuls of fresh basil leaves

SERVES 4

Preheat the oven to 190°C (375°F) Gas 5. Arrange the mini peppers on a large, flat sheet pan and the tomatoes over the top. Sprinkle the chopped garlic over, and then drizzle with olive oil. Season and roast for about 20–25 minutes, until the peppers are soft and starting to char a little at the edges.

Remove the sheet pan from the oven and scatter over the olives. Break the feta into nuggets and scatter them over everything.

For the pesto, put the olive oil, garlic cloves, grated Parmesan and pine nuts into a small food processor (or you could use a jug/pitcher and stick blender). Add the basil leaves and whiz until you have a lightly textured but evenly mixed paste. Season, then dot small spoonfuls of the pesto here and there over the peppers, olives and feta. Serve warm or at room temperature.

SALT-BAKED CELERIAC WITH BLUE CHEESE & HONEY-GLAZED TREVISO

Baking vegetables in a salt crust lifts the humble celeriac/celery root to another level. The flavour permeates through the vegetable, without it tasting over-salty.

for the salt crust
225 g/1³/₄ cups plain/all-purpose flour, plus extra for dusting
400 g/1¹/₂ cups fine sea salt
a big handful of fresh thyme leaves
a handful of freshly chopped rosemary
2 egg whites, lightly beaten

900 g–1 kg/32–35 oz. whole celeriac/celery root
4 treviso chicory/endive, halved from root to tip
5 tbsp olive oil
200 g/7 oz. Gorgonzola cheese (or other punchy blue cheese), broken into small pieces
a handful of very young fresh sage leaves (older leaves will be too bitter)
3 tbsp thick honey
zest and juice of 1 medium orange
freshly ground black pepper
2–3 ratafia biscuits or crisp amaretti biscuits, to serve

SERVES 4

Preheat the oven to 190°C (375°F) Gas 5. Mix the flour and salt together for the salt crust. Stir in the thyme and rosemary. Stir in the egg whites and enough water to bring the mixture together into a smooth, pliable dough. Scatter some flour over a piece of baking parchment and roll the dough out until large enough to cover the entire celeriac/celery root. Sit the celeriac/celery root in the centre of the dough and bring the edges of the parchment up around the sides and push the dough firmly against the skin. Make a small hole in the crust and transfer it to a lightly-floured sheet pan. Bake for about 1 hour 20 minutes, until the skewer slips easily into the centre of the celeriac/celery root.

Remove the celeriac/celery root from the pan, set aside and wipe the pan. Lay the chicory/endive on the pan, cut sides up. Drizzle them with 2 tablespoons of the olive oil and cook for about 20 minutes, until they are soft and golden. Remove the sheet pan from the oven and move the chicory/endive to one side of the pan. Cut the salt crust in half and remove the celeriac/celery root. Peel off the rough skin and cut the flesh into slices. Use three slices to form eight circle-shaped piles on the pan. Divide the Gorgonzola pieces between the piles, scatter over the sage leaves and season with some freshly ground black pepper. Return to the oven for 5–10 minutes, until the cheese has melted. Whisk the remaining olive oil with the honey and orange zest and juice. Remove the sheet pan from the oven, drizzle the orange dressing over the chicory/endive, crumble the ratafia or amaretti biscuits over the celeriac/celery root, and serve.

COURGETTE & SUN-DRIED TOMATO FRITTERS WITH SUMAC KEFALOTYRI

450 g/1 lb. courgettes/zucchinis,
    topped and tailed
scant 1 tsp fine sea salt
80 g/3 oz. sun-dried tomatoes,
    roughly chopped
a generous bunch of spring onions/
    scallions, chopped
2 tbsp fine polenta/cornmeal or semolina
scant 1 tsp baking powder
1 egg, beaten
4–5 tbsp olive oil
150 g/5½ oz. Kefalotyri cheese,
    cut into small cubes
1 tsp ground sumac
freshly ground black pepper
fresh mint leaves and mixed salad, to serve

SERVES 4 (MAKES 8 FRITTERS)

Kefalotyri is a hard cheese from Greece and Cyprus, not dissimilar to halloumi. When oven-baked, it takes on a gorgeous golden colour and has a slightly stringy melting texture and an agreeably salty flavour.

Preheat the oven to 200°C (400°F) Gas 6. Coarsely grate the courgettes/zucchini and put them into a large sieve/strainer. Sprinkle over the salt and leave to stand for about 10 minutes. Squeeze the courgettes/zucchinis to remove as much water as possible, and then transfer them to a large bowl. Add the sun-dried tomato pieces, spring onions/scallions, polenta/cornmeal and baking powder and then stir in the egg until everything is evenly mixed. Season with a little freshly ground black pepper (you shouldn't need to add any additional salt).

Brush a large sheet pan with a little of the oil and drop tablespoonfuls of the mixture over the pan. Bake for 15 minutes. Brush the tops of the fritters with a little of the oil and turn them over. Return to the oven for 5 minutes. In the meantime, toss the cheese cubes with the remaining oil and the sumac, and then arrange them over the fritters. Bake for a further 15 minutes, until the cheese is golden and melted.

Garnish with mint leaves and serve with a mixed salad.

WARM HALLOUMI, FIG & PISTACHIO SALAD

400 g/14 oz. halloumi cheese,
    cut into bite-sized pieces
4 tbsp olive oil
1–2 tsp ras el hanout spice mix
    (see page 77)
8–10 firm, but ripe figs
1–2 tbsp runny honey
2 handfuls of pistachios, crushed
1 tbsp balsamic vinegar
fresh mint leaves, to garnish

SERVES 4

I have never, ever once been able to resist picking at the cheese when I open the oven door and it's there in front of me looking all golden and gorgeous and flecked with spices. Of course, when it's served with warm, sweet figs, drizzled with honey and scattered with pistachios and mint, it's moreish appeal climbs up several notches more, so I really should have more patience, I suppose.

Preheat the oven to 190°C (375°F) Gas 5. Arrange the halloumi pieces in a roasting pan. Drizzle over half of the oil and add the ras el hanout. Carefully toss the cheese and spice mix together so that the cheese is evenly coated. Roast for 10 minutes, until the halloumi is soft and golden. Cut the figs into quarters and arrange them over the pan. Drizzle with the honey and return to the oven for 5–6 minutes, until the figs are warm and soft, but still holding their shape. Scatter over the crushed pistachios. Mix the balsamic vinegar with the remaining olive oil and drizzle it over everything. Garnish with mint leaves and serve warm.

PAPPA AL POMODORO

225 g/8 oz. good sourdough bread
4–5 tbsp olive oil
2 garlic cloves, finely chopped
2 x 400-g/14-oz. cans chopped tomatoes
200 g/7 oz. cherry tomatoes
250 ml/1 cup plus 1 tbsp good-quality
    vegetable stock
1 tsp caster/granulated sugar
a handful of roughly torn basil
sea salt and freshly ground black pepper

to serve
2 tbsp olive oil
fresh basil leaves
50 g/scant 1 cup Parmesan cheese,
    shaved

SERVES 3–4

I fell head over heels with this awesome Italian tomato soup on a week-long press trip to Tuscany. We tucked into a different version every day, often prepared by Tuscan Nonnas, to their secret family recipes. It would definitely be amongst my desert island dishes. This oven-baked version is ace – although I do have to stop myself from nibbling the crisp garlicky bread bits when they come out of the oven.

Preheat the oven to 190°C (375°F) Gas 5. Tear the bread into pieces and put them into a sheet pan. Add the olive oil and garlic and toss well, until the bread is well coated. Bake for about 10 minutes, until the bread is crisp and golden.

Stir in the canned tomatoes, cherry tomatoes, stock and sugar. Season with salt and freshly ground black pepper. Cover with foil and cook for 20 minutes, until the cherry tomatoes have softened. Remove the foil and crush the cherry tomatoes with the tines of a fork. Stir in the torn basil. Return to the oven for 4–5 minutes more.

Drizzle with the oil, scatter with basil leaves and serve with Parmesan shavings.

DAUBE OF AUBERGINES & SHALLOTS
WITH BUTTER BEAN & CHIVE DIP

400 g/14 oz. small shallots
4 tbsp olive oil
2 tbsp caster/granulated sugar
3 medium aubergines/eggplants,
    cut into bite-sized chunks
500 g/18 oz. cherry tomatoes
1 x 400-g/14-oz. can chopped tomatoes
350 ml/1½ cups red wine
3 garlic cloves, finely chopped
1 fresh bay leaf
a bunch of freshly chopped parsley

for the dip
1 x 400-g/14-oz. can butter/lima beans
2 garlic cloves, roughly chopped
3–4 tbsp water
3 tbsp olive oil
juice of 1 lemon
a small bunch of chopped chives

SERVES 4

This dish is adapted from the recipe for Daude de Aubergines in my much-treasured book Mediterranean Cooking, by the incredibly talented Claudia Roden. I thought that caramelized shallots would make a nice addition. The butter/lima bean dip adds extra protein.

Preheat the oven to 190°C (375°F) Gas 5. Peel the shallots, scatter them over the base of a sheet pan and drizzle over the olive oil. Sprinkle over half of the sugar and roast for 15 minutes, until the shallots are turning golden. Add the aubergine/eggplant chunks to the pan. Add the tomatoes and pour over the red wine. Add the garlic and stir in the remaining sugar and the bay leaf. Return the pan to the oven and cook for about 25 minutes more, until the aubergine/eggplant is soft and the sauce has thickened. Remove the bay leaf and stir in the chopped parsley.

For the dip, simply drain and rinse the butter/lima beans and blitz them in a food processor (or use a jug/pitcher and stick blender), with the garlic, water, oil and lemon, until you have a smooth dip. Stir in the chopped chives and serve with the daube.

GREEK POTATO & COURGETTE BAKE
WITH FETA AND FRESH HERBS

This garlic and herb-flecked combination of courgettes, tomatoes and potatoes is the vegetable equivalent of a 'super-group' – what an astoundingly harmonious merger they make. The potatoes are briefly soaked in water, and then rinsed to help remove some of the starch. Don't be tempted to skip on the rinsing. If you merely tip them into a colander or sieve to drain them, you will be flushing all the starchy water back over them, and this will defeat the object of soaking them.

800 g/28 oz. floury potatoes, peeled
    and cut into 3 mm/$\frac{1}{8}$ inch slices
5 ripe tomatoes, roughly chopped
2 fairly large courgettes/zucchinis,
    thinly sliced
4–5 tbsp olive oil
2 garlic cloves, chopped
1 tbsp dried oregano
200 g/7 oz. feta cheese, cut into
    bite-sized chunks
a small bunch of parsley, roughly chopped
sea salt and freshly ground black pepper

SERVES 4

Preheat the oven to 190°C (375°F) Gas 5. Put the potato slices into a large bowl, cover them with cold water and leave them to soak for 10 minutes. Pour them into a colander or large sieve/strainer and rinse them under the cold water tap, until the water runs clear. Dry them on paper towels. Rinse and dry the bowl and return the dried potato slices to it. Add the chopped tomatoes and sliced courgettes/zucchinis. Pour in the olive oil and stir in the chopped garlic and oregano. Season with salt and freshly ground black pepper. Spread the vegetables over a deep sheet pan and cook for about 1 hour, until everything is golden and the potatoes are crisp.

Remove the pan from the oven. Scatter the feta over the vegetables. Sprinkle over the chopped parsley and serve at once.

BAY-SCENTED SUMMER VEGETABLE TIAN

This dish is so simple to make and absolutely sings of summer when it comes out of the oven, bubbling and golden, scenting the air with a gorgeous, aromatic waft of bay. It's a real people-pleaser, and could even be adapted for a vegan diet if the mozzarella was replaced with one of the plant-based cheese substitutes that are readily available now.

2 courgettes/zucchinis, sliced
6 ripe tomatoes, sliced
350 g/12 oz. potatoes, very thinly sliced
80 ml/$\frac{1}{3}$ cup olive oil
1 tsp oregano
2 tsp fresh thyme leaves
350 g/12 oz. mozzarella, sliced
2 small leeks, trimmed and sliced
4–5 fresh bay leaves
sea salt and freshly ground black pepper

a 30 x 17 x 2.5 cm/11$\frac{3}{4}$ x 6$\frac{3}{4}$ x 1 inch
    brownie pan, lightly greased

SERVES 4

Preheat the oven to 190°C (375°F) Gas 5. Put the courgette/zucchini and tomato slices into a large bowl together. Put the potatoes slices into a large sieve, or colander. Rinse the potatoes for a minute or so under the cold water tap, to remove as much starch as possible, then put them into a separate bowl. Divide all but a tablespoon or two of the olive oil between the two bowls, and toss the vegetables to thoroughly coat them, then season each with salt and freshly ground black pepper and add the oregano and thyme leaves. Arrange the vegetables and mozzarella in alternating layers across a sheet pan, standing the slices up on their edges, and packing them quite tightly. Scatter in the sliced leeks as you go. Cut the bay leaves in half and tuck them in here and there. Drizzle over the remaining oil, transfer the sheet pan to the oven and bake for about 50 minutes or so, until the vegetables are cooked and golden. Remove the bay leaves and serve.

OUT OF AFRICA

CARAMELIZED FENNEL & HERITAGE CARROTS
WITH FRESH ORANGES & LEMONY HERB DRESSING

2 bulbs Florence fennel
600 g/21 oz. Heritage carrots
4–5 tbsp olive oil
juice of 1 lemon
2 tsp caster/granulated sugar
4 juicy oranges
sea salt and freshly ground black pepper

for the dressing
100 ml/⅓ cup plus 1 tbsp olive oil
zest and juice of 1 lemon
1 tsp caster/granulated sugar
a large handful of chopped mixed herbs
    (parsley, coriander/cilantro,
    dill, chives, etc.)

SERVES 4

Warm, caramelized fennel and colourful Heritage carrots make magnificent bedfellows to thin slices of fresh juicy oranges. Don't skimp on the herbs.

Preheat the oven to 190°C (375°F) Gas 5. Trim the fennel bulbs, and then cut them in half, from root to tip. Cut each half into three or four wedges. Arrange over a sheet pan. Cut the carrots in half or into quarters along their length, depending on the size of the carrots. Arrange them over the pan with the fennel wedges. Drizzle over the oil and lemon juice and scatter over the sugar. Roast for about 25–30 minutes, until the vegetables are soft and slightly charred at the edges.

In the meantime, top, tail and peel the oranges and cut into thin slices. Mix the oil, lemon juice and sugar together for the dressing, and squeeze in any juice from the end pieces of orange peel. Season with a little salt and black pepper.

Remove the pan from the oven and transfer everything to a platter. Drizzle over the lemon dressing, scatter with the herbs, and serve.

TUNISIAN MECHOUIA SALAD WITH PRESERVED LEMON
& RAS EL HANOUT CAULIFLOWER RICE

3 red onions, cut into wedges
2 red (bell) peppers and 1 yellow (bell)
    pepper, deseeded and cut into strips
350 g/12 oz. cherry tomatoes
2 small aubergines/eggplants, chopped
    into small cubes
2 garlic cloves, chopped
1 large red chilli/chile, deseeded
    and chopped
100 ml/⅓ cup plus 1 tbsp olive oil
1 tbsp sherry vinegar
1 small cauliflower
1 tsp ras el hanout spice mix
¼ preserved lemon
a small bunch of coriander/cilantro,
    chopped
sea salt and freshly ground black pepper

SERVES 4

Mechouia has many variations, but it is essentially a Moroccan salad combining that top notch trio of (bell) peppers, tomatoes and aubergines/eggplants.

Preheat the oven to 190°C (375°F) Gas 5. Put the onion wedges, (bell) peppers and cherry tomatoes on a large, flat sheet pan. Scatter the aubergine/eggplant cubes over the top. Sprinkle over the chopped garlic and chilli/chile, drizzle over about two-thirds of the olive oil, and then transfer the sheet pan to the oven and roast for about 40 minutes – until the vegetables are soft and starting to char at the edges.

Remove the sheet pan from the oven, add the sherry vinegar, and season to taste. Spoon the vegetables onto a pretty platter and keep warm.

Chop the cauliflower into very fine, rice-like pieces. Transfer it to a bowl and add the remaining oil. Add the ras el hanout and toss well to coat. Spoon the mixture over the sheet pan (no need to wash it) and return to the oven for about 10 minutes, until the cauliflower is cooked, but still crunchy.

Remove the pulp from the preserved lemon, rinse the peel and chop it very finely. Stir it into the cooked cauliflower rice. Spoon the cauliflower rice over the mechouia salad and garnish with lots of coriander/cilantro. Serve warm.

SAFFRON CAULIFLOWER STEAKS WITH CANDIED JERUSALEM ARTICHOKES, ROASTED GRAPES, PISTACHIOS & LIME CHERMOULA

Thick slices of cauliflower look so pretty and taste so good when they're given a slick of saffron-infused oil and cooked in the oven. If you've never roasted grapes before, then I think you'll be won over when you try them – especially in this dish, where they perfectly complement the other elements and are set off beautifully with a piquant lime chermoula dressing.

a generous pinch of saffron filaments
juice of 1 lemon
500 g/18 oz. Jerusalem artichokes
1 large cauliflower
50 ml/3½ tbsp olive oil
1 scant tsp paprika
20 g/¾ oz. light brown muscovado sugar
300 g/2 cups small, sweet juicy red grapes
50 g/1¾ oz. pistachios

for the lime chermoula
80 ml/⅓ cup extra virgin olive oil
2 garlic cloves, chopped
1 tsp cumin seeds
1 tsp ground coriander
1 tsp dried chilli/red pepper flakes
a large bunch of coriander/cilantro,
    coarsely chopped
a large bunch of parsley, coarsely chopped
a small handful of mint leaves
zest and juice of 1 large lime

SERVES 4

Preheat the oven to 190°C (375°F) Gas 5. Put the saffron filaments into a small bowl and stir in a tablespoon of just-boiled water. Set aside.

Fill a large bowl with cold water and add the lemon juice. Peel the artichokes, cut into slices, then drop them into the acidulated water to prevent them from browning.

Cut the cauliflower into thick slices to form 'steaks'. Transfer the cauliflower slices to a large, flat sheet pan. Stir 30 ml/2 tablespoons of the olive oil into the saffron infusion and drizzle this over the cauliflower. Sprinkle the slices with paprika. Mix the remaining olive oil with the muscovado sugar. Remove the artichoke slices from the acidulated water and dry briefly on paper towels. Toss them with the oil and sugar mixture. Scatter them over the sheet pan and transfer to the oven. Roast for about 15 minutes, until the vegetables are almost soft.

Cut the grapes into small clusters and arrange them over the pan. Return the pan to the oven and cook for another 10–15 minutes, until the vegetables are soft and golden, and the grape skins are starting to split a little and caramelize. Remove the sheet pan from the oven and scatter over the pistachios.

To make the lime chermoula, simply put all the ingredients into a food processor and blitz to a fairly smooth sauce. Drizzle over the cauliflower steaks, and serve.

HONEY & RAS EL HANOUT ROOTS
WITH PISTACHIOS, POMEGRANATE AND
CORIANDER SHEEPS' MILK YOGURT

Stir the pungent ras el hanout into a little honey, combine it with root vegetables and roast, then add some vibrant green pistachios, juicy pomegranate seeds and a slick of garlic and herb-flecked yogurt – and you could almost be on a camel to Cloud Nine.

300 g/10½ oz. celeriac/celery root,
   peeled and diced
300 g/10½ oz. parsnips, cut into batons
300 g/10½ oz. carrots, cut into batons
150 g/5½ oz. baby turnips, cut into wedges
200 g/7 oz. beetroots/beets, cut into wedges
200 g/7 oz. butternut squash, cut into wedges
200 g/7 oz. shallots, peeled
50 ml/3½ tbsp olive oil
2 tbsp ras el hanout spice mix
1 tbsp runny honey
   (or brown rice syrup for a vegan version)
50 g/1¾ oz. pistachios
seeds from 1 pomegranate
sea salt and freshly ground black pepper
fresh parsley, to garnish

for the ras el hanout spice mix
10 g/⅓ oz. coarsely ground black pepper
10 g/⅓ oz. ground coriander
5 g/1 tbsp ground ginger
5 g/1 tbsp smoked paprika
½ tsp each allspice, ground nutmeg,
   ground turmeric and cayenne pepper
seeds from 2 green cardamom pods
¼ tsp ground cloves
1 tsp dried rose petals

for the yogurt dressing
200 ml/6¾ fl. oz. sheep's milk yogurt
1 garlic clove, peeled and grated
a handful of freshly chopped coriander/
   cilantro

SERVES 4

Preheat the oven to 180°C (350°F) Gas 4. For the ras el hanout spice mix, grind the spices together using a pestle and mortar. Store in a screw-top jar.

Toss the celeriac/celery root, parsnips, carrots, baby turnips, beetroots/beets and butternut squash together in a large sheet pan. Add the shallots. Mix the olive oil with the ras el hanout spice mix, and stir in the honey. Pour this over the vegetables, season with salt and freshly ground black pepper, and toss to coat everything evenly. Roast for about 30–35 minutes, until the vegetables are soft and charred a little here and there. Remove from the oven, transfer to a warm serving dish and scatter over the pistachios and pomegranate seeds.

For the dressing, mix the sheep's milk yogurt with the grated garlic and chopped coriander/cilantro, and spoon a little of the mix here and there. Garnish with fresh parsley and serve warm.

ETHIOPIAN LENTIL CASSEROLE

1 onion, sliced
2 garlic cloves, peeled and chopped
4 tbsp olive oil
2 tbsp Berbere spice mix (see page 82)
2 large carrots
1 large sweet potato (about 250 g/9 oz.),
    peeled and cut into bite-sized chunks
1 x 400-g/14-oz. can chopped tomatoes
4-cm/1$\frac{1}{2}$-inch piece of fresh ginger root,
    grated
450 ml/15 fl. oz. passata/strained tomatoes
800 ml/generous 3$\frac{1}{4}$ cups well-flavoured
    vegetable stock
2 tbsp good-quality tomato ketchup
150 g/scant 1 cup dried red lentils, rinsed
a large handful of fresh baby spinach leaves
a bunch of freshly chopped parsley
chilli/chile oil (see page 25), to serve
    (optional)

SERVES 4

This Ethiopian-influenced lentil stew is great when you're craving something fuss-free and filling but full on flavour. Try not to frown at the idea of adding tomato ketchup to tomato-based dishes – good-quality tomato ketchup puts back the sweetness that can often be lacking in canned tomatoes and passata/strained tomatoes.

Preheat the oven to 190°C (375°F) Gas 5. Scatter the onion over the base of a deep roasting pan. Add the garlic to the pan, drizzle everything with the olive oil and scatter over the berbere spice mix. Give it a good stir to coat everything in the spice mix and cook for 10 minutes.

Cut the carrots into triangular-shaped chunks. Remove the roasting pan from the oven and toss in the carrots and sweet potato. Pour in the chopped tomatoes and stir in the grated ginger. Add the passata/strained tomatoes, stock and tomato ketchup. Stir in the lentils, cover with foil and cook for 30–35 minutes, until the vegetables and lentils are soft and the casserole is nicely thickened.

Stir in the spinach leaves and half of the parsley, and return the pan to the oven for a further 3–4 minutes. Serve with an extra scattering of chopped parsley, and chilli/chile oil, if desired.

AFRICAN PEANUT SOUP

1 large onion, chopped
500 g/18 oz. sweet potatoes, peeled
    and cut into bite-sized chunks
2 red or orange (bell) peppers, deseeded
    and cut into strips
4 tbsp extra virgin olive oil
1 generous tbsp berbere spice mix
    (see page 82)
4-cm/1$\frac{1}{2}$-inch piece of root ginger
2 garlic cloves, finely chopped
1 litre/1 quart vegetable stock
4 tbsp peanut butter
2 tbsp maple syrup
1 x 400-g/14-oz. can butter/lima beans
2 handfuls of kale or other greens
2–3 handfuls of roasted, salted peanuts,
    lightly crushed
a handful of freshly chopped coriander/
    cilantro

SERVES 4

Spicy and satisfying, this gloriously soothing main course soup will warm body and soul on the coldest winter's day. Use a good-quality peanut butter – one that is unsweetened and free from palm oil.

Preheat the oven to 190°C (375°F) Gas 5. Scatter the onion over the base of a deep sheet pan. Add the sweet potatoes and (bell) peppers to the pan. Stir in the oil and berbere spice mix and roast everything for 15 minutes.

Peel the ginger, chop it finely, and add it to the sheet pan with the garlic. Pour in the stock and stir in the peanut butter and maple syrup. Drain and rinse the butter/lima beans, and add them to the pan. Return the pan to the oven and cook for about 20–25 minutes, until the vegetables are soft and the soup has thickened. Add the kale or greens and cook for a further 5 minutes. Remove the pan from the oven, scatter over the crushed peanuts and chopped coriander/cilantro, and serve.

SWEET POTATO, SAFFRON & AUBERGINE CHORBA

2 onions, chopped
2 sweet potatoes (about 400 g/14 oz.), peeled and cut into bite-sized chunks
1 aubergine/eggplant, diced
100 g/3½ oz. cherry tomatoes, sliced
4 tbsp olive oil
2 tbsp ras el hanout spice mix
1 litre/1 quart vegetable stock
a generous pinch of saffron filaments
100 g/½ cup plus 1 tbsp quick-cook spelt or basmati rice
1 x 400-g/14-oz. can chickpeas
a handful of freshly chopped coriander/cilantro

SERVES 4

Chorba is a hearty soup or stew, not dissimilar to harira, and is popular in many north African countries. I like to serve it with some thick, natural/plain yogurt, a slick of chilli/chile oil and some good crusty bread.

Preheat the oven to 190°C (375°F) Gas 5. Add the onions and the sweet potatoes to a large sheet pan. Add the aubergine/eggplant and cherry tomatoes. Drizzle the oil over the vegetables and stir in the ras el hanout spice, so that everything is well coated. Transfer the pan to the oven and roast for 20–25 minutes, until the vegetables have taken on a golden colour.

Pour the stock into the pan and add the saffron and the spelt (or rice). Drain and rinse the chickpeas, add to the pan, and give everything a good stir round. Return the pan to the oven and cook for a further 25–30 minutes, until the spelt (or rice) is soft and the soup has thickened. Scatter with freshly chopped coriander/cilantro and serve.

HARIRA SOUP WITH SAFFRON & CHILLI HUMMUS

2 onions, coarsely chopped
2 sticks/stalks celery, diced
2 large carrots, diced
4 tbsp olive oil
1 tsp ground ginger
1 tbsp ground coriander
1 tbsp ground cumin
2 tsp ground turmeric
2 garlic cloves, chopped
100 g/½ cup plus 2 tbsp green or Puy lentils
1 x 400-g/14-oz. can chopped tomatoes
1 litre/1 quart vegetable stock
1 x 400-g/14-oz. can chickpeas
40 g/1½ oz. dried spaghetti or vermicelli noodles
a bunch of freshly chopped coriander/cilantro

for the saffron & chilli/chili hummus
50 ml/3½ tbsp just-boiled water
a pinch of saffron filaments
1 x 400-g/14-oz. can chickpeas
2 generous tbsp tahini paste
2 garlic cloves, roughly chopped
juice of 1 lemon
½ tsp chilli/red pepper flakes
3–4 tbsp olive oil
sea salt and freshly ground black pepper

SERVES 4

Sometimes referred to as the national soup of Morocco, harira is frequently eaten during the Muslim fasting period of Ramadan. Typically, it does contain meat – often lamb – but is every bit as delicious when made without. Built on a rich, spicy tomato base and chock-full of vegetables, pulses and pasta, it makes a hearty meal in itself. I've teamed it with a glorious saffron and chilli hummus.

Preheat the oven to 190°C (375°F) Gas 5. Scatter the onions over a deep sheet pan. Add the celery and carrots to the pan. Drizzle over the oil and stir in the ground spices. Roast for 15 minutes, until the vegetables are starting to soften.

Remove the pan from the oven and stir in the garlic, lentils, chopped tomatoes and stock. Drain and rinse the chickpeas and add them to the pan. Return the pan to the oven and cook for a further 20 minutes. Break the spaghetti or vermicelli noodles into 2 cm/¾ inch lengths, and stir into the soup. Return to the oven and cook for a further 10 minutes, until the pasta is soft. Garnish with freshly chopped coriander/cilantro.

For the hummus, mix the water and saffron together and leave for 10 minutes (or longer if you have time) to infuse. Drain and rinse the chickpeas and pop them in a food processor (or use a bowl and stick blender). Add the tahini paste and pour in the saffron and water. Add the garlic, lemon juice, chilli flakes and oil. Blitz to a smooth paste and season to taste. Serve.

BERBERE ROASTED CAULIFLOWER
WITH APRICOTS, PINE NUTS & MUHAMMARA

Berbere is a punchy hot spice mix from Ethiopia – making your own means you can adjust the heat to suit. Muhammara is a glorious, dip-into or dollop-on invention that hails from Aleppo in Syria, but is now popular all across the whole Levantine area.

for the muhammara
2 red (bell) peppers, deseeded
  and cut into strips
3 tbsp olive oil
1 tsp ground cumin
50 g/½ cup walnut pieces
1 garlic clove, finely chopped
30 g/½ cup fresh breadcrumbs
1 tbsp pomegranate molasses
1 tbsp good-quality tomato ketchup
1 tsp dried chilli/red pepper flakes
sea salt and freshly ground black pepper

for the berbere spice mix
30 g/1 oz. chilli/red pepper flakes
8 g/¼ oz. flaked sea salt
8 g/¼ oz. coarsely ground black pepper
7 g/scant ¼ oz. ground cumin
7 g/scant ¼ oz. coriander seeds
2 g fenugreek powder
1 g ground ginger
⅓ tsp allspice
⅓ tsp ground cloves
⅓ tsp ground nutmeg
seeds from 2 green cardamom pods

for the cauliflower
1 good-sized cauliflower
3–4 tbsp olive oil
1½ tbsp berbere spice mix (see above)
50 g/scant ½ cup toasted pine nuts/kernals
200 g/1⅓ cups dried apricots, halved

to serve
2 tbsp pomegranate molasses
3 tbsp olive oil
a handful of freshly chopped coriander/cilantro
a small handful of freshly chopped parsley
mint leaves, to garnish

SERVES 4

Preheat the oven to 190°C (375°F) Gas 5. To make the muhammara, toss the red (bell) peppers with 2 tbsp of the oil and the cumin and arrange the strips over a large sheet pan. Roast for about 20 minutes, until softened and slightly charred.

Transfer to a blender and whiz to a purée. Add the walnuts, garlic, breadcrumbs, pomegranate molasses, ketchup, chilli/red pepper flakes and remaining oil and whiz again, until you have a lightly textured purée with the consistency of whipped cream. If the mixture is a little too thick, add some warm water. Season and set aside.

For the berbere spice mix, grind the spices together using a pestle and mortar, until you have a lightly textured powder.

For the cauliflower, break the cauliflower into small florets and toss in a bowl with the olive oil and Berbere spice mix.

Spread over the sheet pan used for the (bell) peppers and roast for about 15 minutes, until the cauliflower is cooked, but still has a little bite. Scatter over the pine nuts/kernels and apricots and return to the oven for a few minutes to warm through.

Stir the pomegranate molasses and oil together and spoon over the cauliflower. Scatter with the freshly chopped herbs and mint leaves, and serve with the muhammara.

BAHARAT AUBERGINE STEAKS,
WITH FETA, DATES, PHYSALIS, STICKY DATE DRESSING & TAHINI YOGURT

Baharat is the Turkish word for 'spice', but it is also a mixture used in Middle Eastern cuisine. It's an aromatic and fairly kick-ass combination of cayenne pepper, paprika, cumin, coriander, nutmeg, cloves and cardamom and is easily bought as a ready-made blend, but is great to make at home too. It transforms oven-baked aubergine/eggplant slices into something incredible, and when they're served alongside caramel-sweet dates, salty feta and slightly sharp physalis berries and a sesame paste and yogurt sauce, the result is quite positively, *a coup de maitre* (which is French for something like 'a stroke of genius'). A peppery rocket/arugula salad makes a great accompaniment.

1–2 tbsp baharat spice mix
50 ml/3½ tbsp olive oil
1 aubergine/eggplant, thinly sliced
100 g/⅔ cup medjool dates, stoned/
    pitted and halved
3 tbsp date syrup
200 g/7 oz. feta cheese
100 g/3½ oz. fresh physalis berries,
    halved
mint leaves, to garnish

for the tahini yogurt
120 g/generous ½ cup full-fat natural/
    plain yogurt
1–2 garlic cloves, finely grated
1 generous tbsp tahini paste
juice of ½ lemon

SERVES 3-4

Preheat the oven to 190°C (375°F) Gas 5. Mix the baharat spice with the olive oil and paint this liberally over the aubergine/eggplant slices. Arrange them on a sheet pan and bake for about 15–20 minutes, until they are soft and a rich golden brown.

In the meantime, mix the dates with the date syrup and a splash of hot water and leave them to plump up while the aubergine/eggplant is in the oven.

Remove the pan from the oven. Break the feta cheese into chunks and scatter it over the aubergine/eggplant slices. Arrange the dates here and there, drizzle the syrup over the aubergine/eggplant slices, and return everything to the oven for just 5 minutes, to warm through.

In the meantime, for the tahini yogurt, beat the yogurt, garlic, tahini paste and lemon juice together until smooth. Set aside.

Remove the sheet pan from the oven, and dot the physalis halves here and there. Garnish with fresh mint leaves and serve warm, with the tahini yogurt.

CHARRED TURNIP, RADISH & RED ONION SALAD
WITH ROASTED GARLIC (NO EGG) MAYONNAISE

400 g/14 oz. radishes
400 g/14 oz. small turnips, cut into quarters
4 red onions, cut into wedges
1 whole bulb fresh garlic
4 tbsp olive oil
1 tsp caster/granulated sugar
1 tbsp fresh thyme leaves
150 g/5½ oz. red chicory/endive
dill fronds, to garnish

for the (no egg) mayonnaise
2 tbsp chickpea water (aquafaba)
1 scant tbsp Dijon mustard
2 tbsp cider vinegar
150 ml/²/3 cup sunflower oil
sea salt

SERVES 4

Turnips probably don't have the biggest fan club, but when roasted, the transformation is spectacular.

Preheat the oven to 200°C (400°F) Gas 6. Scatter the radishes, turnips and red onions over a large sheet pan. Cut the whole garlic bulb in half horizontally and lay it in the corner of the sheet pan, cut sides up. Drizzle everything with the olive oil. Sprinkle the radishes, turnips and onions with the sugar, but avoid the garlic. Scatter over the thyme leaves. Bake for 35 minutes, until the vegetables are soft and golden and slightly charred. Remove from the oven, leave to cool slightly, and transfer to a pretty platter. Arrange the red chicory/endive leaves here and there and garnish with dill fronds.

For the (no egg) mayonnaise, put the chickpea water, mustard and cider vinegar into a jug and add a pinch of salt. Blitz with a stick blender until mixed. Slowly pour in the sunflower oil, until the mixture has emulsified and thickened. Squeeze the roasted garlic out of the crispy little compartments of skin into the mixture and blitz again until well mixed. Serve with the charred turnip and radish salad.

BAKED KHORASAN WHEAT WITH BARBERRIES,
SAFFRON, PRESERVED LEMON & ROSE PETALS

2 leeks, trimmed sliced
3 tbsp olive oil
250 g/1½ cups khorasan wheat
700 ml/3 cups vegetable stock
a pinch of saffron filaments
2 tbsp dried barberries
¼ preserved lemon
100 g/3½ oz. fresh tomatoes, finely chopped
300 g/10½ oz. cauliflower, broken into florets
300 g/10½ oz. broccoli, broken into florets
2 handfuls of kale, chopped
1–2 tsp dried rose petals
freshly chopped mixed herbs
    (parsley, dill, mint and coriander/cilantro)

for the preserved lemon dressing
¼ preserved lemon
50 ml/3½ tbsp olive oil
juice of 1 lemon
1 tsp caster/granulated sugar

SERVES 4

Khorasan wheat, or kamut, as it is also known makes a great grain-based salad. It makes a moreish lunch when partnered with some simple leaves.

For the dressing, discard the flesh of the preserved lemon, rinse the peel and chop it finely. Add it to the olive oil, lemon juice and sugar and whisk until fully combined.

Preheat the oven to 190°C (375°F) Gas 5. Scatter the leeks over the base of a sheet pan. Drizzle over the oil and cook for 10 minutes, until the leeks have started to soften slightly. Add the khorasan wheat to the pan and stir in the stock, saffron and barberries. Cover with foil and transfer to the oven. Cook for 25 minutes, until the wheat is soft and most of the liquid has been absorbed. Discard the flesh from the preserved lemon, rinse the peel and chop finely.

Remove the foil from the sheet pan and stir the preserved lemon, tomatoes and cauliflower and broccoli florets into the wheat, along with half of the chopped kale. Scatter the remaining kale over the top. Return to the oven for 10 minutes, until the vegetables are soft, but still have a little bite, and the kale on the top is crisp and golden. Scatter with dried rose petals and chopped mixed herbs and serve with the preserved lemon dressing.

ASIA & THE EAST

CAULIFLOWER, SULTANA & MANGO SALAD
WITH LENTILS & TURMERIC, GINGER & MAPLE DRESSING

The fresh turmeric dressing takes this dish to another level. Neon-orange turmeric root has a more zippy flavour than dried turmeric. Its increasing popularity means that it is now fairly readily available.

1 large cauliflower (500 g/18 oz. trimmed weight in florets)
6 tbsp olive oil
1 tbsp ground coriander
1 tbsp ground cumin
1 tbsp fennel seeds
1 tsp dried chilli/red pepper flakes
1 tbsp demerara/turbinado sugar
2 red (bell) peppers, deseeded and cut into strips
3 red onions, cut into wedges
200 g/7 oz. cherry tomatoes, halved
1 x 400-g/14-oz. can black beluga lentils, drained and rinsed
2–3 tbsp sultanas/golden raisins
1 small, ripe mango, peeled, pitted and diced

a bunch of fresh coriander/cilantro, roughly chopped
sea salt and freshly ground black pepper

for the dressing
25 g/1 oz. fresh turmeric, peeled and finely grated
2 cm/³⁄₄ inch knob of fresh ginger, peeled and finely grated
2 garlic cloves, finely grated
2 tbsp tahini paste
zest and juice of 1 lime
50 ml/3¹⁄₂ tbsp water
4 tbsp olive oil
1 tsp caster/granulated sugar
1–2 tbsp maple syrup

SERVES 4

Preheat the oven to 190°C (375°F) Gas 5. Break the cauliflower into florets. Pour the oil into a large bowl, and add the coriander, cumin, fennel seeds, chilli/red pepper flakes and sugar. Give everything a good stir, season with salt and pepper, and toss the cauliflower florets into the mixture to coat. Spread them over a large sheet pan. Scatter the red (bell) peppers, onion wedges and cherry tomatoes over the sheet pan and mix. Roast for 20–25 minutes (give everything a stir halfway through the cooking time), until the cauliflower is cooked but still has some bite.

Stir the lentils gently into the roasted vegetables. Return the sheet pan to the oven for 5 minutes, until the lentils are just heated through. Remove the pan from the oven and scatter over the sultanas/raisins. Scatter the mango over the salad and garnish with the coriander/cilantro. For the dressing, put the grated turmeric and ginger into a bowl. Add all the remaining ingredients and whisk together until smooth. Season to taste, drizzle over the salad and serve.

SPICED TOMATOES WITH PANEER & PEAS

450 g/1 lb. paneer, cut into 1-cm/¹⁄₂-in. dice
3 tbsp olive oil
2 tsp ground cumin
2 tsp ground coriander
1 tsp ground turmeric

for the sauce
2 onions, sliced
4 large ripe tomatoes, roughly chopped
500 g/18 oz. passata/strained tomatoes
5-cm/2-inch piece of root of ginger, chopped
2 garlic cloves, finely chopped
50 g/¹⁄₂ cup ground almonds
300 g/scant 2¹⁄₂ cups frozen peas
a handful of chopped coriander/cilantro
extra chopped coriander/cilantro, mango chutney and naan bread, to serve

SERVES 4

Paneer is really useful to keep in the fridge for vegetarians. When you stir it into pungent spice mixes and lip-smacking sauces, it happily seems to slurp up the flavours amazingly well. I love this with mango chutney and peshwari naan.

Preheat the oven to 190°C (375°F) Gas 5. Put the paneer into a large bowl. Add the oil, cumin, coriander and turmeric and give everything a good stir to coat the paneer. Transfer to a deep sheet pan. Roast for 10 minutes.

Meanwhile, for the sauce, add the onions to the bowl you were using for the paneer. Add the tomatoes and pour in the passata/strained tomatoes. Stir the ginger into the tomato mix together with the garlic. Add the ground almonds and mix.

Remove the paneer from the oven and pour over the tomato mix. Return to the oven for 20 minutes. Stir in the peas and chopped coriander/cilantro and return to the oven for 5 minutes more. Serve with extra chopped coriander/cilantro, mango chutney and naan bread for scooping.

TAMARIND & ROSEMARY SWEET POTATOES
WITH SHALLOTS & TOASTED HAZELNUTS

1 kg/35 oz. sweet potatoes, peeled
  and chopped into chunks
300 g/10½ oz. shallots
40 g/1½ oz. tamarind paste
40 g/1½ oz. brown rice syrup
40 ml/scant 3 tbsp olive oil
2 tbsp finely chopped rosemary
100 g/3½ oz. whole hazelnuts,
  lightly crushed

SERVES 4

This top-notch combo makes a really good side dish, but could be served as a main alongside a green salad or some lightly cooked greens. Although its actually vegan-friendly, you could happily feed it to the most staunch carnivore and I'm certain they wouldn't miss the meat for a minute.

Preheat the oven to 190°C (375°F) Gas 5. Put the sweet potatoes into a large bowl. Peel the shallots and add to the bowl. Mix the tamarind paste with the brown rice syrup, olive oil and rosemary. Add to the bowl and toss everything together. Arrange over a large sheet pan. Roast for 15 minutes. Scatter over the hazelnuts and cook for a further 15 minutes, until the vegetables are soft and golden. Serve straight away.

ALOO GOBI, ROASTED POTATO & CAULIFLOWER CURRY

2 red onions, sliced
2 garlic cloves, finely chopped
400 g/14 oz. cherry tomatoes, roughly
  chopped
500 g/18 oz. new potatoes, cut into wedges
4–5 tbsp olive oil
2 tbsp panch phoran (see page 96)
1 tbsp cumin seeds
1 tsp dreied chilli/red pepper flakes
1 medium cauliflower
1 generous tsp ground turmeric
a handful of cashew nuts

a handful of baby spinach leaves, washed
sea salt and freshly ground black pepper
chopped coriander/cilantro, to serve

for the mint and garlic yogurt
150 g/scant ¾ cup full-fat natural/plain
  yogurt (or substitute coconut yogurt
  for vegans)
1 garlic clove, finely grated
a small bunch of fresh mint,
  roughly chopped

SERVES 4

This moreish dish is very loosely based on the Northern Indian curry Aloo Gobi. I hope that I will be forgiven by Aloo Gobi aficionados for freestyling.

Preheat the oven to 190°C (375°F) Gas 5. Scatter the onions over a large, flat roasting pan, together with the garlic, tomatoes and potato wedges. Drizzle in half of the olive oil, scatter over the panch phoran, cumin seeds and chilli/red pepper flakes and toss everything together. Roast for about 25 minutes until the potatoes are starting to brown.

Break the cauliflower into florets and put them into a bowl. Add the remaining olive oil and the turmeric. Season with salt and freshly ground black pepper and toss everything together to coat. Remove the pan from the oven and add the cauliflower to the pan. Give everything a gentle stir to mix, scatter over the cashew nuts, and then return to the oven for about 15 minutes, until the cauliflower is golden and cooked, but still slightly crisp. Gently fold in the spinach leaves, which should quickly wilt in the residual heat – no need to return to the oven. Garnish with freshly chopped coriander/cilantro.

Mix everything for the mint and garlic yogurt together in a bowl. Season with a little salt and black pepper and serve with the roasted potato and cauliflower curry.

SALT-BAKED HERITAGE BEETROOT & MANGO LETTUCE CUPS WITH NERIGOMA DRESSING

800 g/4 cups coarse sea salt
3 egg whites
4 candy-striped and yellow beetroots/beets
50 ml/3¹/₂ tbsp olive oil
juice of 2 limes
1 tsp caster/granulated sugar
1 small red onion, sliced
1 large, ripe but firm tomato,
    roughly chopped
1 medium, ripe mango, peeled, pitted
    and diced
a small of handful of freshly chopped
    coriander/cilantro
sea salt and freshly ground black pepper
iceberg or Little Gem lettuce cups
fresh mint leaves, to garnish

for the nerigoma dressing
4 tbsp nerigoma
zest and juice of 1 lime
1 fat garlic clove, finely grated
3–4 tbsp water

SERVES 4

Salt-baking seems to intensify the sweetness of beetroot/beet. If you can manage to find different coloured beetroots/beets, it makes this a very beautiful dish. Served in lettuce cups, it makes a very special dinner party starter.

Preheat the oven to 190°C (375°F) Gas 5. Put the salt into a large bowl and mix in the egg whites. Spread about a third of the mixture in a thin layer on a lined sheet pan. Place the beetroots/beets close together, and then pat the remaining salt mixture over the beetroots/beets to cover them. Bake for about 1 hour, until the beetroots/beets are soft when tested with the point of a knife.

Meanwhile, mix the olive oil, lime juice and sugar in a large bowl. Season.

When the beetroots/beets are cooked, give the salt crust a good thwack with a rolling pin, and remove them. Once the beetroots/beets are cool enough, gently peel away the skin and cut them into dice. Drop them into the lime dressing whilst they are still warm, and leave to cool completely.

Add the onion, tomato and mango to the dressing and stir in the chopped coriander/cilantro.

Whisk all the ingredients for the nerigoma dressing together. Carefully peel away layers of the lettuce to make cups and fill them with the beetroot/beet mixture. Garnish with mint leaves, and serve with the nerigoma dressing.

BAKED SWEET POTATOES
WITH MISO BUTTER, CHIVES & BLACK SESAME SEEDS

4 medium sweet potatoes
3 tbsp olive oil
1–2 tbsp fresh thyme leaves

for the miso butter
150 g/1¹/₄ sticks butter, softened
20 g/³/₄ oz. white miso paste
a bunch of chives, chopped
1 tbsp black sesame seeds
rocket/arugula salad, to serve

SERVES 4

Miso adds the most glorious, rich, umami flavour to anything it touches. When you beat a small amount into creamy butter and let it melt over hot sweet potatoes you'll find your taste buds dancing the sprightliest of tangos.

Preheat the oven to 190°C (375°F) Gas 5. Wash the sweet potatoes and cut them in half from tip to tip. Lay them on a sheet pan, cut side up, score the flesh lightly with a diamond pattern, and drizzle them with oil. Scatter over the thyme leaves. Transfer to the oven and roast for about 35–40 minutes, until very soft.

Beat the butter and miso paste together, until evenly combined. Stir in half of the chopped chives. Remove the sweet potatoes from the oven and mash the centres of each roughly, using a fork. Spoon over some miso butter, and sprinkle over the black sesame seeds and remaining chives. Serve hot with a salad.

CRISPY BENGALI 5 SPICE POTATOES
WITH SPRING ONIONS & CHILLI & CORIANDER RAITA

for the panch phoran spice mix
10 g/¹/₃ oz. nigella (black onion) seeds
10 g/¹/₃ oz. cumin seeds
10 g/¹/₃ oz. black mustard seeds
10 g/¹/₃ oz. fenugreek seeds
10 g/¹/₃ oz. fennel seeds

500 g/18 oz. floury potatoes
50 g/1³/₄ oz. panch phoran spice mix
4–5 tbsp olive oil
a large bunch of spring onions/scallions,
   sliced
1–2 red chillies/chiles, deseeded and sliced
sea salt flakes and freshly ground black pepper

for the raita
200 g/scant 1 cup full fat plain/natural
   yogurt
2 garlic cloves, grated
a handful of freshly chopped coriander/cilantro

SERVES 4

Panch phoran is an amazing aromatic mix of five whole spices that originally hails from Bengal and Eastern India. It adds the wow factor to all manner of dishes – from hearty curries to simple steamed veg. You can buy it as a ready-made mix, but it's such a doddle to make, you may just as well rustle up your own.

Preheat the oven to 190°C (375°F) Gas 5. Combine all the whole seeds together for the spice mix.

Peel the potatoes, and cut them into small dice – about 15 mm/⁵/₈ inch square. Put them into a bowl and add the panch phoran spice mix. Add the oil, and then toss everything together until the potatoes are evenly coated in the spices. Arrange them evenly over a large, flat sheet pan and roast for about 50 minutes or so – until they are golden and crisp. Remove from the oven and season with salt flakes. Scatter the spring onions/scallions and chillies/chiles over the potatoes.

Meanwhile, put the yogurt into a bowl and stir in the grated garlic and chopped coriander/cilantro. Season with a few salt flakes and a little freshly ground black pepper. Serve alongside the Bengali 5 spice potatoes.

CRISPY RICE WITH SOY & GINGER TEMPEH

200 g/7 oz. tempeh
5 tbsp dark soy sauce
1 tbsp sesame oil
1 tsp caster/granulated sugar
30 g/1 oz. fresh ginger, finely grated
2 garlic cloves, finely grated
200 g/generous 1 cup basmati rice
3 tbsp olive oil
a bunch of spring onions/scallions, chopped
a bunch of freshly chopped coriander/cilantro
1 tbsp white sesame seeds, to garnish

SERVES 4

At first glance, soy-rice-speckled tempeh seems neither attractive nor inspiring – but its saving grace is that it does absorb strong flavours and marinades very well. It responds well to baking too, so this is one of those dishes that die hard meat-eaters are really very pleasantly surprised by.

Preheat the oven to 190°C (375°F) Gas 5. Cut the tempeh into slices. Mix the soy sauce, sesame oil and sugar together in a large bowl. Stir in the grated ginger and garlic. Toss the tempeh slices in the mixture and leave to marinate.

Rinse the rice under running water, until the water runs clear. Scatter it over the base of a lined, deep sheet pan. Pour in 800 ml/scant 3¹/₂ cups water and bake for about 30 minutes, until the water has been absorbed and the rice is cooked. Remove the pan from the oven and drizzle over the olive oil. Remove the tempeh from the marinade and lay it in a row down the centre of the rice. Return to the oven and bake for about 10 minutes, until the tempeh is hot and the rice is crisp. Scatter over the spring onions/scallions, coriander/cilantro and sesame seeds, and serve.

FRESH LIME, VEGETABLE & COCONUT CURRY

I love Thai coconut curries, but more often than not, standard Thai curry pastes usually contain dried shrimps or fish sauce – so I've come up with this delicious and easily made alternative paste. It helps if you have a food processor, or mini chopper, but you could also make the paste using a pestle and mortar. The vegetables don't need to be cooked for too long, otherwise they will lose their lovely vibrant colour and crispy texture. If you're using long-stemmed broccoli, opt for young, smaller stems.

for the curry paste
45 g/1½ oz. knob of fresh ginger, peeled
2 garlic cloves, peeled
1 stalk lemongrass, trimmed
3 kaffir lime leaves
1 tbsp ground coriander
1 tbsp ground cumin
1 scant tbsp dried chilli/ red pepper flakes
1 tbsp coconut oil
1–2 tbsp warm water
a bunch of fresh coriander/ cilantro

for the curry
2 x 400-ml/14-fl. oz. cans full fat coconut milk
100 ml/⅓ cup plus 1 tbsp well-flavoured vegetable stock
1 tbsp demerara/turbinado sugar

100 g/3½ oz. cherry tomatoes, roughly chopped
1 yellow (bell) pepper, deseeded and cut into strips
400 g/14 oz. mixed young vegetables (sugar snap peas, green/French beans, young, long-stem broccoli, baby sweetcorn, etc.)
a small bunch of fresh coriander/ cilantro, roughly chopped
zest and juice of 1 large lime

to serve
a handful of cashew nuts
a bunch of spring onions/ scallions, thinly sliced

SERVES 4

To make the curry paste, roughly chop the ginger, garlic and lemongrass and add them to a food processor or mini chopper and whiz until finely chopped (or bash them using a pestle and mortar if preferred). Add the lime leaves, ground coriander, cumin, chilli/red pepper flakes and coconut oil. Pour in the warm water and blitz everything to a paste. Add the coriander/cilantro and whiz again until everything is ground down and evenly mixed.

Preheat the oven to 180°C (350°F) Gas 4. For the curry, pour the coconut milk and stock into a deep roasting pan and stir in the curry paste and sugar. Cover with foil and cook for 15 minutes.

Remove the roasting pan from the oven, give everything a good stir and add the chopped tomatoes, (bell) pepper strips and prepared vegetables (cut the baby/sweet corn in half from top to bottom, if using). Replace the foil and cook for 10 minutes or so, until the vegetables are just soft but retain their bright colours.

Stir in the fresh coriander/cilantro and add the lime zest and juice. Serve straight away, scattered with cashews and spring onions/scallions.

TURMERIC MACADAMIAS

Macadamia nuts have a beautiful, buttery texture. When they're roasted with a light scattering of turmeric, they become absolutely irresistible. I find it very easy to polish off a whole batch this size on my own.

150 g/5½ oz. macadamias
1 tbsp olive oil
1 tsp ground turmeric
1 tsp brown rice syrup
sea salt flakes

SERVES 2-3

Preheat the oven to 190°C (375°F) Gas 5. Put the macadamias into a large bowl and add the olive oil, turmeric and brown rice syrup. Season with some salt flakes. Bake for about 4–5 minutes, until golden and roasted. Store well away from temptation.

CHICKPEA & ALMOND CURRY

This makes a fabulous, reasonably inexpensive but very healthy weekday supper and is equally suitable for both vegetarians and anyone following a plant-based diet. If you drain the water from the can of chickpeas, and save it – you can use it to make the aquafaba meringues on page 140. It might sound a little crazy, but trust me – chickpea water makes great, billowy-crisp vegan-friendly meringues rather than having to use egg whites. Honestly!!!! Serve the curry with chapatis and mango chutney – and possibly yogurt if you're so inclined.

2 onions, sliced
4–5 tbsp olive oil
2 tsp garam masala
1 tsp ground turmeric
1 tsp ground coriander
1 tsp ground cumin
1 tsp dried chilli/red pepper flakes
60 g/2¼ oz. fresh ginger
2 garlic cloves, finely chopped
2 x 400-g/14-oz. cans chopped tomatoes

2 x 400-g/14-oz. cans chickpeas, drained and rinsed
2 tbsp good-quality tomato ketchup
80 g/¾ cup ground almonds
freshly chopped coriander/cilantro leaves
1 red chilli/chile, deseeded and sliced, to garnish

SERVES 4

Preheat the oven to 190°C (375°F) Gas 5. Scatter the onion slices over the base of a deep sheet pan and drizzle with the olive oil. Add the garam masala, turmeric, ground coriander, cumin and chilli/red pepper flakes. Stir to coat the onions in the spices. Roast for 10 minutes. Peel the ginger and cut it into julienne. Remove the pan from the oven and add the ginger and chopped garlic. Stir in the chopped tomatoes, chickpeas, tomato ketchup and ground almonds. Return the pan to the oven and cook for about 20–25 minutes, until the sauce is lovely and thickened. Garnish with chopped coriander/cilantro and red chilli/chile slices.

EASY OVEN DAL

This comforting dal is quick and easy to make and cooks beautifully by itself in the oven. If you're like me and tend to have some fresh ginger in the fridge, canned tomatoes in the cupboard, and have a few basic spices – then it's a real storecupboard supper. I like it with a scattering of extra chilli/red pepper flakes and a slick of yogurt, but if you prefer to make it dairy-free, then some fruity chutney makes a great match too.

1 onion, sliced
5 tbsp olive oil
1 tsp ground cumin
1 tsp ground coriander
1 tsp ground turmeric
60 g/2¼ oz. fresh ginger
1 tsp dried chilli/red pepper flakes (or to taste)
1 tsp caster/granulated sugar
2 garlic cloves, chopped
300 g/1¾ cups dried red lentils, rinsed

800 ml/generous 3¼ cups water
1 x 400-g/14-oz. can chopped tomatoes
sea salt flakes and freshly ground black pepper
extra chilli/red pepper flakes, natural/plain yogurt, and/or chutney, to serve

SERVES 4

Preheat the oven to 190°C (375°F) Gas 5. Scatter the onion over the base of a deep sheet pan. Drizzle the olive oil over and stir in the cumin, coriander and turmeric. Transfer to the oven and cook for 10 minutes. In the meantime, peel the ginger and cut it into julienne. Remove the sheet pan from the oven and stir in the ginger julienne, the chilli/red pepper flakes, sugar and chopped garlic. Stir in the red lentils, water and canned tomatoes. Cover the sheet pan with foil, and cook for about 30–35 minutes, until the lentils are soft and the dal has a nice creamy texture (you may have to add a little more water if it seems to be getting a little too dry). Season with salt flakes and freshly ground black pepper, and serve with extra chilli/ red pepper flakes and yogurt or chutney (or both!).

STICKY SESAME AUBERGINE WITH GOCHUJANG KETCHUP

2 medium aubergines/eggplants
2 tbsp sesame oil
2 tbsp olive oil
4 cm/1½ inch piece of ginger root,
    peeled and grated
4 tbsp ketjap manis
    (thick, sweet Indonesian soy sauce)
120 ml/½ cup dark soy sauce
4 tsp gochujang paste
2 tsp caster/granulated sugar
3 garlic cloves, chopped
2–3 tbsp sesame seeds
a bunch of spring onions/scallions, chopped

for the gochujang ketchup
4 tbsp gochujang paste
4 tbsp good-quality tomato ketchup

4 pitta breads, warmed, to serve
shredded lettuce, to serve

SERVES 4

Gochujang paste is a massive favourite of mine – I love its glossy, piquant richness and the deep relish it adds to so many dishes. Here, I've used it in an easy marinade for bite-sized chunks of aubergine/eggplant, which absorb the glorious flavours and transform into toothsome loveliness. Spoon into warm pitta bread, with crisp shredded lettuce and gochujang ketchup.

Preheat the oven to 190°C (375°F) Gas 5. Cut the aubergines/eggplants into bite-sized cubes and transfer them to a large bowl. In a separate bowl, mix the sesame oil, olive oil, grated ginger, ketjap manis, soy sauce, 4 teaspoons gochujang paste, sugar and garlic. Stir everything together and pour the mixture over the aubergine/eggplant cubes. Toss to coat everything well. Spoon the aubergine/eggplant evenly over a large, flat sheet pan and roast for about 25–30 minutes, until the aubergine/eggplant is cooked. Scatter over the sesame seeds and chopped spring onions/scallions.

To make the gochujang ketchup, simply mix the 4 tablespoons gochujang paste with the tomato ketchup in a small bowl.

Scoop the aubergine/eggplant mixture into warmed pitta breads, and add shredded lettuce and gochujang ketchup, as desired.

EDAMAME, NOODLE & SPRING ONION OMELETTE

Noodles make a lovely addition to this Asian-inspired, baked omelette. I serve it for a super-speedy light lunch, cut into pretty triangles, accompanied by a juicy tomato salad and shredded lettuce.

300 g/10½ oz. fresh fine
    rice noodles
8 large eggs, beaten
3 tbsp dark soy sauce
1 tsp sesame oil
150 g/5½ oz. frozen edamame
    beans, defrosted
a large bunch of spring onions/
    scallions, chopped
a bunch of dill, chopped
a bunch of chives, chopped
a bunch of parsley, chopped
sea salt and freshly ground
    black pepper

for the tomato salad
300 g/10½ oz. baby plum
    tomatoes, halved
2 tbsp extra virgin olive oil

shredded iceberg lettuce,
    to serve
extra soy sauce, for drizzling
a 30 x 17 x 2.5 cm/11¾ x 6¾
    x 1 inch brownie pan, lightly
    greased and lined with baking
    parchment

SERVES 4

Preheat the oven to 190°C (375°F) Gas 5. Lay the noodles out evenly over the base of the prepared brownie pan. Beat the eggs together in a large bowl and add the soy sauce and sesame oil. Season with a little salt and freshly ground black pepper and stir in the beans, chopped spring onions/scallions and half of all the herbs. Pour the mixture over the noodles. Transfer to the oven and cook for 10 minutes, until the omelette is just set. Cut into squares, then triangles and scatter over the remaining herbs. For the fresh tomato salad, combine the tomatoes and oil season to taste. Serve the omelette alongside the salad and some shredded lettuce. Offer extra soy sauce, for drizzling.

SHIITAKE MUSHROOM & PURPLE SPROUTING BROCCOLI BROTH
WITH SMOKED TOFU

Shiitake mushrooms have a subtle, slightly smoky flavour and a silky texture when cooked and they're lovely in this light broth. I've used Japanese brown rice miso paste to add a gorgeous whisper of umami. Definitely one that will have you feeling virtuous, delighted and satisfied in equal measure.

1 red onion, finely chopped
50 g/1¾ oz. knob of fresh ginger, peeled
2 garlic cloves, peeled
1.2 litres/5 cups good-quality vegetable stock
50 g/1¾ oz. brown rice miso paste
250 g/9 oz. shiitake mushrooms
300 g/10½ oz. purple sprouting broccoli
200 g/7 oz. smoked tofu, cut into strips
300 g/10½ oz. pak choi/bok choy,
    cut into thick slices
a bunch of spring onions/scallions,
    cut into slices diagonally
1–2 red chillies/chiles, deseeded and sliced
fresh mint leaves, to garnish

SERVES 4

Preheat the oven to 190°C (375°F) Gas 5. Scatter the onion across the base of a deep sheet pan. Cut the ginger into thin julienne and finely chop the garlic. Add them both to the pan containing the onion. Pour in the vegetable stock and stir in the brown rice miso paste and the mushrooms. Cover with foil and cook for 15 minutes.

Trim the purple sprouting broccoli, separate it into small florets and peel the stems to remove any tough or stringy skin. Add it to the pan, re-cover with the foil, and cook for a further 10 minutes. Remove the foil and add the tofu strips and pak choi/bok choy. Return to the oven for another 5 minutes.

Scatter the broth with the spring onions/scallions, chillies/chiles and fresh mint leaves and serve at once.

THE AMERICAS

HASSELBACK COQUINA SQUASH
WITH CHILLI MAPLE GLAZE & SALT FLAKES

You may well have made hasselback potatoes – the gorgeous potatoes that are cooked whole, but thinly sliced along their length almost all the way through, so that the slices fan out slightly as they cook and become crisp and golden. Here, I've used the same method to cook coquina squash (a close relative of the butternut) and glazed it with a sticky-sweet-slightly-spicy combination of maple syrup, soy sauce and chilli/chile.

A great trick for cutting the thin slices without inadvertently cutting all the way through, is to lay a chopstick along both lengths of the squash, so that the knife will go no further once it reaches the sticks.

1 coquina squash
50 ml/3½ tbsp maple syrup
20 ml/4 tsp Indonesian soy sauce
　(ketjap manis)
25 ml/5 tsp dark soy sauce
1 tsp dried chilli/red pepper flakes
a bunch of spring onions/scallions,
　diagonally sliced
a handful of fresh coriander/cilantro,
　roughly chopped

SERVES 3-4

Preheat the oven to 190°C (375°F) Gas 5. Cut the squash in half from base to top, and scoop out the seeds. Remove the peel using a vegetable peeler. Cut each half widthways into thin slices, stopping a little way short of cutting all the way through so that the squash halves are still intact. Lay them on a lightly oiled sheet pan. Mix the maple syrup, soy sauces and chilli/red pepper flakes together and brush generously over the squash halves, making sure to get plenty in between each slice. Bake for about 30–35 minutes, basting regularly, until the squash is cooked through and has a beautiful shiny glaze.

Transfer to a platter and scatter over the spring onions/scallions and coriander/cilantro. Serve hot.

MEXICAN VEGETABLE & KIDNEY BEAN BAKE WITH AVOCADO HOLLANDAISE

This is a meat-free chilli/chili that will tempt carnivores, vegetarians and vegans alike. It doesn't pack too much of a punch, making it family-friendly, but chilli/chili-fiends could add some dried chilli/hot red pepper flakes, a slick of the chilli oil on page 25, or even a scattering of some freshly chopped chilli/chile. The avocado 'hollandaise' lifts the whole dish to another level, so do make sure to serve the two together.

1 onion, chopped
3 celery stalks, chopped
2 garlic cloves, finely chopped
3 sweet potatoes, peeled and diced
2 carrots, diced
2 yellow (bell) peppers, deseeded
  and cut into strips
1 red (bell) pepper, deseeded
  and cut into strips
250 g/9 oz. chestnut mushrooms, sliced
450 g/1 lb. cherry tomatoes
4–5 tbsp olive oil
2 tsp ground cumin
2 tsp ground coriander
2 tsp chilli/chili powder
2 tsp caster/granulated sugar
600 ml/2½ cups passata/strained tomatoes
2 tbsp good-quality tomato ketchup
400-g/14-oz. can red kidney beans,
  drained and rinsed
2 handfuls of fresh baby spinach leaves
a handful of freshly chopped coriander/
  cilantro
sea salt and freshly ground black pepper

for the avocado hollandaise
1 large, ripe avocado
juice of ½ lemon
50 ml/3½ tbsp water
2 tbsp olive oil

SERVES 4

Preheat the oven to 180°C (350°F) Gas 4. Scatter the onion, celery and garlic into a deep sheet pan.

Add the sweet potatoes, carrots, (bell) peppers, mushrooms and cherry tomatoes to the pan. Drizzle in the olive oil, add the spices and sugar, season with salt and freshly ground black pepper and roast for 20–35 minutes, until the vegetables have started to soften and brown. Remove from the oven and stir in the passata/strained tomotoes and ketchup. Cook for a further 30 minutes. Remove from the oven, stir in the kidney beans, spinach and half of the coriander/cilantro. Return to the oven for about 5 minutes, until the spinach is just wilted. Scatter over the remaining coriander/cilantro.

In the meantime, make the avocado hollandaise. Peel the avocado and remove the pit. Chop the flesh and pop it into the bowl of a blender (alternatively, use a jug/pitcher and a stick blender). Add the lemon juice, water and olive oil and whiz to a smooth purée. Season to taste, transfer to a small bowl and serve alongside the vegetable and kidney bean bake.

ROASTED PEPPER, SWEETCORN & BLACK-EYED BEAN WRAPS WITH CHIPOTLE DRESSING & AVOCADO SPREAD

2 red (bell) peppers, deseeded
    and cut into strips
2 orange (bell) peppers, deseeded
    and cut into strips
3 tbsp olive oil
2 corn on the cob/ears of corn
1 x 400-g/14-oz. can black eyed beans
2 ripe avocados, peeled and pitted
juice of 1 lime
1 small red chilli/chile, deseeded
    and finely chopped
4 flour tortillas
a large bunch of spring onions/scallions, sliced
a small bunch of coriander/cilantro
sea salt and freshly ground black pepper
soured/sour cream, to serve

for the dressing
2 tbsp chipotle paste
2 tbsp olive oil
1 tbsp red wine vinegar
2 tsp caster/granulated sugar

SERVES 4

I have the most gargantuan soft spot for sunny coloured roasted (bell) peppers. They morph into the juiciest, sweetest delights and make a fantastic filling for these moreish tortilla wraps, when partnered with sweet, crunchy corn, black eyed beans and ripe avocado. They're nice with the roasted chilli jam on page 121 too.

Preheat the oven to 190°C (375°F) Gas 5. Scatter the (bell) peppers over a sheet pan, drizzle over the oil and roast for 15 minutes, until they are starting to soften and char. Cut the kernels from the sweetcorn/corn cobs, add them to the pan with the pepper strips and cook for a further 10 minutes. Drain and rinse the beans, and add them to the pan to warm through for 4–5 minutes.

Meanwhile, mash the avocado flesh in a bowl and add the lime juice and chopped chilli/chile. Season to taste.

For the dressing, whisk the chipotle paste, oil, vinegar and sugar together and season to taste.

Spread each of the tortillas with some of the avocado spread and pile with some of the bean mixture. Drizzle over some of the dressing, and scatter with a few chopped spring onions/scallions and some coriander/cilantro leaves. Roll up and serve with soured/sour cream.

MOLE-STYLE MUSHROOMS

2 dried ancho chillies/chiles
2 onions, sliced
3 tbsp olive oil
2 tbsp ground cumin
1 tbsp dried oregano
1–2 tbsp smoked paprika
1 tbsp fennel seeds
2 x 400-g/14-oz. cans chopped tomatoes
50 g/1/2 cup ground almonds
1 kg/35 oz. mushrooms, stalks removed
    (I use a mix of white and chestnut)
200 ml/3/4–1 cup chilli/chile soaking water
300 ml/11/4 cups well-flavoured vegetable stock
2 tbsp caster/granulated sugar
100 g/31/2 oz. sultanas or raisins
80 g/3 oz. 70% dark/bittersweet chocolate

SERVES 4

Rich, chilli/chile-charged mole sauces are super-popular in Mexican cuisine – they often include dark chocolate to give them a unique and delicious tang.

Preheat the oven to 190°C (375°F) Gas 5. Put the dried ancho chillies/chiles into a jug/pitcher and cover with water. Leave to soak for about 30 minutes.

Meanwhile, scatter the onions into the base of a deep sheet pan. Pour over the oil and stir in the cumin, oregano, paprika and fennel seeds. Roast for 10–15 minutes, until the onions have started to soften.

Remove the ancho chillies/chiles from the soaking water (reserve the water), cut off the tops (no need to remove the seeds), and blitz them in a food processor with the tomatoes and ground almonds. Pour the mixture into the softened onions, add the mushrooms, the chilli/chile soaking water and stock. Stir in the sugar and sultanas or raisins. Break the chocolate into small pieces and add it to the pan too. Cook for about 45 minutes, until the sauce is thickened. Serve.

LOADED BLACK BEAN & SWEETCORN NACHOS

1 x 200 g/7 oz. bag tortilla chips
200 g/7 oz. cherry tomatoes,
    coarsely chopped
300-g/10½-oz. can sweetcorn/
    corn kernels, drained
1 x 400-g/14-oz. can black beans,
    drained and rinsed
1 x small jar jalapeño peppers,
    drained and sliced
a bunch of spring onions/scallions,
    thinly sliced
200 g/2¼ cups extra mature Cheddar
    cheese, grated
soured/sour cream, to serve

SERVES 4

I find that nachos marry particularly well with a gin and tonic and are much more exciting than simply crunching through a packet of crisps on a Saturday night. I'm saying that there's enough for four people here, but in fairness, that would probably be four very restrained, polite people – so you might want to double up on the quantities. I've been known to polish off a whole batch to myself.

Preheat the oven to 190°C (375°F) Gas 5. Scatter a handful of tortilla chips over the base of a large sheet pan. Scatter over a handful of chopped cherry tomatoes, then some sweetcorn/corn kernels and some black beans. Dot with jalapeño pepper slices, scatter over some spring onions/scallions and then sprinkle the cheese generously over the top. Repeat these layers until you have used everything up. Transfer to the oven and bake for 4–5 minutes, until the cheese is melted and gooey. Serve with soured/sour cream.

PORTABELLO MUSHROOM BURGER
WITH ROASTED ONIONS & CREOLE SWEET POTATO FRIES

4 large Portabello mushrooms
90 ml/⅓ cup olive oil
2 garlic cloves, finely chopped
a small bunch of freshly chopped parsley
2 handfuls of roughly chopped walnuts
2–3 large sweet potatoes
1 tbsp Creole spice blend/seasoning
3 red onions
2 tsp fresh thyme leaves
4 brioche burger buns
2 handfuls of shredded iceberg lettuce
3 tomatoes, sliced
2 small avocados, pitted and sliced
sea salt and freshly ground black pepper

to serve
mayonnaise (or the egg-free mayonnaise
    on page 86 or 117)
sriracha sauce or roasted chilli jam
    from page 121

SERVES 4

If you've never roasted a big, succulent, garlicky Portabello mushroom in the oven and eaten it hot, in a bun – juices dripping as you bite into it – then you've been missing out on something very special. If said mushroom happens to be stuffed with crunchy walnuts and served in a buttery brioche bun, loaded up with lettuce, tomatoes and avocado, then things have just shot up another notch.

Preheat the oven to 190°C (375°F) Gas 5. Lay the mushrooms out (gill sides up), along one side of a large, flat sheet pan. Mix half of the olive oil with the garlic, parsley and walnuts and season to taste. Spoon the mixture over the mushrooms. Peel the sweet potatoes, and cut them into medium-thickness chips/fries. Toss with half of the remaining oil and the Creole spices. Spoon the chips/fries onto the sheet pan. Peel and slice the onions horizontally, and lay these on the sheet pan. Drizzle with the remaining olive oil and scatter with the thyme leaves. Transfer the sheet pan to the oven and roast for about 25 minutes or so, until the mushrooms are soft and the sweet potato chips/fries are golden.

Cut the brioche buns in half and fill with the lettuce, tomatoes, sliced avocados, and the roasted mushrooms and onions. Serve with mayonnaise, sriracha sauce or roasted chilli jam, and the Creole spiced chips/fries.

JERK VEGGIE SKEWERS WITH CELERIAC, SULTANA & CAPER SALAD

1 red, 1 yellow and 1 orange (bell) pepper, deseeded and cut into strips
2 red onions, cut into wedges
2 medium courgettes/zucchinis, thickly sliced
200 g/7 oz. baby button mushrooms
200 g/7 oz. baby plum or cherry tomatoes
6 tbsp olive oil
3 tbsp jerk spice mix
2 tsp light muscovado sugar

for the salad
1 small celeriac/celery root
2 crisp eating apples
50 g/1/3 cup sultanas/golden raisins
1 tbsp capers, drained
a small bunch of freshly chopped parsley
1 quantity egg-free mayonnaise
   (see page 86)

8 long, wooden skewers

SERVES 4

I've teamed the zippy skewers up with a dreamy salad of crisp celeriac/celery root and apple, peppered with salty capers and sweet plump sultanas/golden raisins. Simplicity at its delicious best.

Preheat the oven to 200°C (400°F) Gas 6. Push the prepared vegetables, mushrooms and tomatoes onto the skewers, alternating them as you go. Lay them on a large, flat sheet pan.

Mix the oil, jerk spice mix and sugar together in a bowl and brush this over the vegetables. Transfer the pan to the oven and roast for 15–20 minutes, until the vegetables are soft, but retaining a little bite.

To make the salad, peel the celeriac/celery root, cut it into slices and then into fine julienne. Transfer to a large bowl. Core the apples, cut them into similar sized strips and add to the bowl, together with the sultanas/raisins and capers.

Add the egg-free mayonnaise to the celeriac/celery root and apple salad and stir in the chopped parsley. Serve alongside the veggie skewers.

TRINIDADIAN VEGETABLE PELAU

1 onion, chopped
2 large carrots, diced
2 celery stalks, diced
1 yellow (bell) pepper, deseeded and diced
1 red (bell) pepper, deseeded and diced
20 g/1 tbsp plus 1 tsp light brown
   muscovado sugar
3 tbsp olive oil
2 garlic cloves, grated
50 g/1¾ oz. ginger root, peeled and grated
300 g/1¾ cups wholegrain basmati rice
2 x 400-g/14-oz. cans coconut milk
1 x 400-g/14-oz. can black-eyed beans
1 tsp fresh thyme leaves
1 red chilli/chile, deseeded and chopped
a bunch of spring onions/scallions, chopped
a bunch of coriander/cilantro, chopped
sea salt and freshly ground black pepper

SERVES 4

Based on the traditional Trinidadian rice dish, pelau, this dish has an irresistible hint of sweetness that contrasts beautifully with the kick of ginger and chilli/chile.

Preheat the oven to 190°C (375°F) Gas 5. Scatter the chopped onion over the base of a deep sheet pan. Add the carrots, celery and (bell) peppers to the pan. Sprinkle over the muscovado sugar and stir in the olive oil. Transfer the pan to the oven and cook for 15 minutes.

Remove the pan from the oven and add the garlic and ginger. Put the rice into a sieve, rinse it until the water runs clear and add it to the pan. Stir in the coconut milk and 400 ml/scant 1¾ cups water. Drain and rinse the beans and add them to the pelau with the thyme leaves and chopped chilli/chile. Return the sheet pan to the oven and cook for a further 40 minutes or so, until the rice is cooked and all the liquid is absorbed. Season to taste, stir in the spring onions/scallions and coriander/cilantro, and serve with extra chopped chilli/chile, if desired.

TEX-MEX VEGGIE TACOS WITH FRESH
TOMATO SALSA & CHIPOTLE MAYONNAISE

This dish is a riot of colour, flavours and textures. You could fill the tacos before you serve them, but it creates such a lovely, relaxed dining experience when you lay everything out so that everyone can dive in and fill their own.

1 large sweet potato, peeled and
   cut into chunks
1 small butternut squash, peeled,
   deseeded and cut into chunks
1 red (bell) pepper, deseeded and diced
2 corn on the cob/ears of corn
4 tbsp olive oil
2 garlic cloves, grated
1 tbsp paprika
1 tbsp freshly chopped rosemary
1 x 400-g/14-oz. can red kidney beans
8 crunchy taco shells
a small bunch of freshly chopped parsley

for the tomato salsa
200 g/7 oz. cherry tomatoes
1 small red onion
juice of 1 lime
a small bunch of freshly chopped
   coriander/cilantro
a handful of fresh mint leaves, roughly torn

for the chipotle mayonnaise
2 tsp chipotle paste
1 quantity egg-free mayonnaise
   (see page 86)

2 handfuls of shredded iceberg lettuce,
   to serve

SERVES 4

Preheat the oven to 190°C (375°F) Gas 5. Scatter the sweet potato, butternut squash and (bell) pepper over the base of a large sheet pan. Stand the corn cobs/ears on a board and remove the corn using a sharp knife and a downward motion. Scatter the sweetcorn/corn kernels over the vegetables in the pan. Drizzle everything with the olive oil, sprinkle in the grated garlic, paprika and freshly chopped rosemary. Transfer to the oven and roast for about 25 minutes, until the sweet potato and squash are soft.

Remove the pan from the oven. Drain and rinse the kidney beans and add to the vegetables, then push everything up the pan slightly, so that you can tuck the taco shells across one end. Return the pan to the oven for about 3–4 minutes, until the tacos are crisp and the beans are heated through. Stir the chopped parsley into the vegetables.

For the tomato salsa, coarsely chop the tomatoes and put them into a bowl. Peel and thinly slice the onion and stir it into the tomatoes. Squeeze in the lime juice and add the coriander/cilantro and torn mint leaves.

For the chipotle mayonnaise, mix the chipotle paste and mayonnaise together.

Place a little shredded lettuce into the base of each taco, pile with the vegetable mix and some salsa, then drizzle with a little chipotle mayonnaise – or lay everything out on a platter and invite everyone to fill their own.

OVEN-ROASTED CHILLI JAM

Sticky, spicy, and bursting with vibrant colour and flavour, this chilli/chile jam makes a great accompaniment to a whole host of different dishes. If I have the oven on and some tomatoes that need using, there's every chance I'll end up putting on a batch of this lovely condiment because somehow, my fridge always feels more complete when I know I have some in there, even though it seems to disappear as quickly as I make it.

1 kg/35 oz. fresh tomatoes
5–6 red chillies/chiles, stalks removed
100 ml/1/3 cup plus 1 tbsp white wine vinegar
6-cm/2½-inch piece of root ginger
300 g/1½ cups caster/granulated sugar
3 tbsp olive oil

SERVES 6-8

Preheat the oven to 190°C (375°F) Gas 5. Put the tomatoes and chillies/chiles into a food processor and blitz until really finely chopped. Pour them into the bottom of a large, deep sheet pan. Stir in the white wine vinegar.

Peel the ginger and chop it very finely. Stir it with the sugar into the tomato mixture and transfer the sheet pan to the oven. Cook for about 1 hour, stirring occasionally, until the tomato mixture is sticky and jam-like. Add the olive oil, and give the mixture a final stir. Pour into a sterilized airtight jar, seal and cool, then store in the fridge for up to a couple of weeks.

ROASTED RED PEPPER, CHILLI & ALMOND DIP
WITH TORTILLA CRISPS

Roasted (bell) pepper yumminess again – this time whizzed into a zippy almond dip and served alongside crunchy tortilla crisps/chips. Piri-piri seasoning is nice on the tortilla crisps/chips too.

2 red (bell) peppers, deseeded
  and cut into strips
200 g/7 oz. cherry tomatoes
3 tbsp olive oil
50 g/½ cup ground almonds
2 garlic cloves, chopped
1 tsp dried chilli/red pepper flakes
sea salt flakes

for the tortilla crisps/chips
4 flour tortillas
2–3 tbsp olive oil
1 tsp paprika

SERVES 4

Preheat the oven to 190°C (375°F) Gas 5. Scatter the (bell) peppers over a large, flat sheet pan lined with baking parchment along with the cherry tomatoes. Drizzle with the oil, add a scattering of salt flakes and roast for about 20 minutes or so, until the (bell) peppers are cooked and beginning to char, and the tomatoes are soft. Transfer everything to a food processor (you could use a bowl and a stick blender if preferred), making sure to add all the lovely tomatoey juices. Add the ground almonds, chopped garlic and chilli/red pepper flakes and blitz until you have a fairly smooth dip. Meanwhile, for the tortilla crisps/chips remove and discard the baking parchment from the sheet pan. Cut the flour tortillas into bite-sized triangular-ish pieces (I always end up with a few wacky shapes too). Put them into a bowl and toss with the olive oil, paprika and some salt flakes. Spread them over the sheet pan and pop them into the oven for about 4–5 minutes, until they are golden and crisp. Transfer the dip and the crisps/chips to separate bowls and enjoy!

CHILLI CARAMEL NUTS

200 g/1½–2 cups mixed nuts (whole
   almonds, pecans, cashews, pistachios)
2 tbsp olive oil
2 tbsp brown rice syrup
1 tbsp maple syrup
1 generous tsp mild paprika
1 tsp dried chilli/red pepper flakes
sea salt

SERVES 2–4

These crunchy, savoury-sweet chilli/chile-spiked nuts are seriously special. I love to serve them with drinks when friends come over – but they're great to munch on whilst watching a movie too.

Put the mixed nuts into a large bowl. Add the olive oil, brown rice syrup, maple syrup and paprika. Stir in the chilli/red pepper flakes and a sprinkling of salt. Bake for 10 minutes, stirring a couple of times as they cook. Leave to cool and try not to eat them all before serving.

CREOLE SQUASH WITH ROASTED SWEETCORN & TOMATOES

Zippy Creole spices do wonderful things to roasted roots. They add a special magnificence to wedges of butternut squash. Cooking is all about creating harmony between ingredients – and in this lovely dish, the sweetness of the corn, and the juiciness of the tomatoes complement the squash to create a really awesome dish. A generous slick of soured/sour cream makes a gorgeous addition, but if you're aiming to keep it dairy-free, I'm sure you'll be delighted with it just as it is.

4–5 tbsp olive oil
1–2 tbsp Creole spice blend/seasoning
1 medium butternut squash, deseeded,
   peeled and cut into wedges
2 corn on the cob/ears of corn
300 g/10½ oz. cherry tomatoes
sea salt and freshly ground black pepper
a bunch of freshly chopped chives, for
   sprinkling

SERVES 2–4

Preheat the oven to 190°C (375°F) Gas 5. Pour the oil into a large bowl and stir in the Creole spices. Add the squash wedges. Cut the corn cobs into slices about 1 cm/½ inch thick. Add to the bowl too. Give everything a good stir round, until the vegetables are coated with the spiced oil. Season and arrange over a sheet pan. Transfer the pan to the oven and roast for 10 minutes. Scatter the whole cherry tomatoes randomly but evenly over the sheet pan and return to the oven for a further 25 minutes or so, until everything is golden and cooked.

Remove from the oven, sprinkle over the chives and serve.

SWEET TREATS

PEACH & RASPBERRY GRATIN

6 sweet, ripe (but firm) peaches
juice of 1 small orange
250 g/generous 1 cup mascarpone
50 g/¼ cup caster/superfine sugar
seeds from 1 cardamom pod
seeds from 1 vanilla pod
3 eggs, separated
200 g/1½ cups raspberries
1–2 tsp soft light muscovado sugar
mint leaves, to decorate

SERVES 4

Sweet, perfumed peaches with a gorgeous mascarpone custard that hints delicately, yet deliciously of cardamom. Please don't be tempted to add any more than the seeds from one little green cardamom pod, or you'll end up spoiling it.

Preheat the oven to 180°C (350°F) Gas 4. Cut the peaches in half, remove the pits and arrange them on a deep sheet pan, cut side up. Sprinkle with the orange juice. Bake for 8–10 minutes, until slightly softened.

Meanwhile, mix the mascarpone with the caster/superfine sugar, cardamom seeds and vanilla seeds. Whisk in the egg yolks.

Set one of the egg whites aside for another dish, and whisk the other two until firm peaks form. Fold the egg whites into the mascarpone mix. Drop spoonfuls of the mixture here and there on the sheet pan. Scatter over the raspberries and sprinkle with muscovado sugar. Return the sheet pan to the oven for a further 5–8 minutes. Decorate with mint leaves, and serve warm or at room temperature.

BASTED BABY PINEAPPLES
WITH COCONUT & CHOCOLATE CRUMBS

4 sweet, ripe baby pineapples
200 ml/¾–1 cup dark rum
150 g/¾ cup dark brown muscovado sugar
2 tsp vanilla bean paste
1 tsp ground cinnamon

for the chocolate crumbs
30 g/1 oz. coconut oil
50 g/½ cup ground almonds
60 g/5 tbsp caster/superfine sugar
20 g/¾ oz. cocoa powder
25 g/3 tbsp plain/all-purpose flour
pieces of fresh coconut and fresh mint
    leaves, to decorate

a 30 x 17 x 2.5 cm/11¾ x 6¾ x 1 inch
    brownie pan, lightly greased and lined
    with baking parchment

SERVES 4

Baby pineapples make a pretty and pleasing dessert because they're generally very ripe and sweet and everyone gets their own whole fuzzy-topped pineapple. If you can't get hold of the baby ones, you could slice two larger ones into wedges.

Preheat the oven to 190°C (375°F) Gas 5. Cut the woody bases from the pineapples and, using a very sharp knife, peel them carefully in a downwards motion from beneath the plume of leaves to the base.

Mix the rum, brown sugar, vanilla bean paste and cinnamon together in a large bowl, and sit the peeled pineapples in the mixture to macerate.

Meanwhile, blitz all the ingredients for the chocolate crumbs together in a food processor. Scatter the mixture over the prepared brownie pan and bake for 15–20 minutes, until crisp. Remove from the oven and transfer the crumbs to a small bowl. Re-line the pan with a clean piece of baking parchment, remove the pineapples from the rum mix and stand them upright on the pan. Pour the remaining rum mix into the pan and baste the pineapples. Transfer to the oven and cook for about 20 minutes or so – basting with the rum liquid from time to time. Remove the pineapples from the oven and leave to cool a little before transferring to a serving platter. Spoon over any of the remaining (now syrupy) rum mixture, serve with the chocolate crumbs and coconut pieces, and decorate with fresh mint leaves.

STICKY SPICED PUMPKIN & STEM GINGER SQUARES

150 g/5½ oz. peeled weight pumpkin or
butternut squash flesh (or use canned)
300 g/2¼ cups plain/all-purpose flour
1 tsp ground ginger
1 tsp ground cinnamon
2 tsp baking powder
1 tsp bicarbonate of/baking soda
150 ml/²/₃ cup sunflower oil
150 ml/²/₃ cup brown rice syrup
250 g/1¼ cups dark muscovado sugar
2 eggs, beaten
100 ml/¹/₃ cup plus 1 tbsp whole milk
200 g/7 oz. crystallized ginger, coarsely
chopped
3–4 tbsp brown rice syrup, for glazing

a 30 x 17 x 2.5 cm/11¾ x 6¾ x 1 inch
brownie pan, lightly greased and lined
with baking parchment

MAKES 15

These squares of light-as-air, beautifully flavoured cake are an absolute joy for ginger lovers. Canned pumpkin makes a fine substitute for fresh if you're a little short of time. Pile up the squares on a plate and serve with your favourite brew.

Preheat the oven to 170°C (325°F) Gas 3. Cut the peeled pumpkin into small dice and place in a sheet pan.

Drizzle with a little water and cover with foil. Bake for about 20–25 minutes, until the flesh is very soft. Spoon into a food processor and blend until you have a purée (add a tiny bit of water if you need to). Give the pan a rinse and then brush it all over with a little oil and line with baking parchment.

Meanwhile, mix the flour with the spices, baking powder and bicarbonate of/baking soda in a bowl. Set aside.

Beat the sunflower oil and brown rice syrup together with the sugar. Add the eggs and milk and beat until everything is smooth. Stir in the pumpkin purée and dry ingredients. Add the ginger pieces and stir until evenly combined.

Spoon the mixture into the lined brownie pan and bake for about 30 minutes or so, until the cake springs back when gently prodded. Leave to cool for a few minutes and then gently brush over the rice syrup to glaze. Cut and serve.

PECAN & PRETZEL SQUARES

for the base
125 g/9 tbsp butter
200 g/1½ cups plain/all-purpose flour
50 g/¼ cup caster/superfine sugar

for the topping
6 eggs, beaten
200 g/²/₃ cup maple syrup
50 g/¼ cup dark brown muscovado sugar
2 tsp vanilla bean paste
1 tsp ground cinnamon
250 g/9 oz. pecan nuts, coarsely chopped
50 g/1¾ oz. plain pretzels

a 30 x 17 x 2.5 cm/11¾ x 6¾ x 1 inch
brownie pan, lightly greased and lined
with baking parchment

MAKES 15

If you like pretzels and you have a soft spot for pecan pie, I think you'll happily declare these sticky-sweet-salty squares a real winner. They're so easy to make too – no pastry rolling and blind-baking, just a lovely, buttery press-into-the-pan base that cooks until crisp and goes beautifully with the indulgent nutty topping.

Preheat the oven to 180°C (350°F) Gas 4. For the base, rub the butter into the flour until the mixture resembles fine breadcrumbs. Add the sugar, and draw everything together into a soft ball. Press it into the base of the prepared brownie pan and bake for 10–15 minutes, until golden and firm.

For the topping, beat the eggs, maple syrup and sugar together. Stir in the vanilla bean paste and cinnamon.

Once the base is cooked, immediately scatter over the chopped pecan nuts whilst it is still hot. Break the pretzels in half and scatter them over the nuts. Spoon the maple syrup mixture evenly over everything and return to the oven for a further 25–30 minutes, until the topping is set. Remove from the oven and leave to cool in the pan, before cutting into squares.

WHITE CHOCOLATE, ALMOND & RASPBERRY RIPPLE BROWNIES

These white chocolate brownies seem to spread supreme joy to all who try them, although I feel they're slightly responsible for the spreading of my hips too, as I am unable to stop at eating just one. I'm also very guilty of trimming off the crusts and eating those too – although I do believe that crusts don't count, especially if you eat them standing up.

200 g/1¾ sticks butter, melted
150 g/5½ oz. white chocolate, melted
400 g/2 cups caster/superfine sugar
4 eggs, beaten
100 g/¾ cup plain/all-purpose flour
200 g/2 cups ground almonds
½ tsp baking powder

200 g/7 oz. raspberries
1 tbsp caster/superfine sugar
50 g/1¾ oz. white chocolate, melted, to decorate

a 30 x 17 x 2.5 cm/11¾ x 6¾ x 1 inch brownie pan, lightly greased and lined with baking parchment

MAKES 15

Preheat the oven to 170°C (325°F) Gas 3. Pour the melted butter and white chocolate into a large bowl and stir in the 400 g/2 cups of sugar. Beat in the eggs. Add the flour, ground almonds and baking powder and beat together until everything is evenly incorporated. Pour the mixture into the prepared brownie pan.

Push the raspberries through a fine sieve/strainer into a bowl, and stir the 1 tablespoon sugar into the purée. Spoon the purée over the top of the brownie mix in generous swirls. Bake for about 45 minutes–1 hour, until golden and firm when gently prodded in the centre with your index finger.

Drizzle over the extra melted white chocolate to decorate, and leave to cool in the pan. Trim the edges and eat them (standing up), cut the brownies into squares and serve.

VEGAN BROWNIES

I won't lie to you – it did take me a few attempts to reach a level of squidginess that I was really happy with here – but I got there in the end! These lovely, dark, dense brownies are sure to delight chocolate-loving vegans, but I think they will also surprise conventional brownie fans too. They're fab served warm, with a good dairy-free ice cream – but are equally nice served cold with a cuppa.

200 g/7 oz. dark/bittersweet chocolate, melted
250 ml /1 cup plus 1 tbsp just-boiled water
100 ml/⅓ cup plus 1 tbsp sunflower oil
375 g/2 cups minus 2 tbsp light brown muscovado sugar
1 tsp cider vinegar
2 tsp vanilla bean paste

175 g/1⅓ cups plain/all-purpose flour
½ tsp baking powder

a 30 x 17 x 2.5 cm/11¾ x 6¾ x 1 inch brownie pan, lightly greased and lined with baking parchment

MAKES 15

Preheat the oven to 170°C (325°F) Gas 3. Pour the melted chocolate into a large bowl and slowly whisk in the just-boiled water. Whisk in the sunflower oil. Beat in the muscovado sugar, and then add the cider vinegar and vanilla bean paste. Stir in the flour and baking powder.

Pour the mixture into the prepared pan, and bake for about 45 minutes, until the top of the brownie feels squidgy but set. Leave to cool in the pan, before cutting into squares. Store in an airtight tin, making sure to separate any layers with baking parchment if necessary.

LEMON YOGURT SQUARES

These luscious zingy-light lemon squares are absolute winners...BUT...I must ask rather nicely (but very firmly) that you resist the urge to replace the full-fat Greek yogurt with a low-fat or 0% concoction, because, without the teeniest, tiniest shred of a doubt, the recipe simply won't be the same. Baking relies on accuracy much more than any other form of cooking. The flavour and consistency of a lower fat yogurt would really spoil the recipe and would also save very little on calories.

for the base
125 g/½ cup plus 1 tbsp butter, softened
200 g/1½ cups plain/all-purpose flour
50 g/¼ cup caster/superfine sugar

for the topping
500 g/1 lb. 2 oz. full-fat Greek yogurt
300 g/1½ cups caster/superfine sugar
zest of 2 lemons and juice of 4
4 eggs
2 egg yolks
80 g/⅔ cup plain/all-purpose flour

a 30 x 17 x 2.5 cm/11¾ x 6¾ x 1 inch
  brownie pan, lightly greased and lined
  with baking parchment

MAKES 15

Preheat the oven to 180°C (350°F) Gas 4. For the base, rub the butter, flour and sugar together until the butter is evenly incorporated and the mixture resembles fine breadcrumbs. Bring the mixture together to form a ball, and press it evenly over the base of the prepared brownie pan. Transfer the pan to the oven and bake for 15 minutes, until golden and firm.

Meanwhile, for the topping, beat the yogurt, sugar and lemon zest and juice together in a large bowl. Add the eggs, egg yolks and flour, and beat together until smooth.

Remove the shortbread base from the oven and immediately pour over the yogurt mixture in an even layer. Return the pan to the oven and bake for a further 30 minutes, until the topping is set and golden. Leave to cool in the pan, and then cut into squares to serve.

APRICOT FRANGIPANE PUFF SQUARES

Sticky glazed squares of apricot-and-frangipane-topped puff pastry. Yes please.
Thickly whipped fridge-cold cream is a bonus. Resistance is futile.

320 g/11½ oz. good-quality,
  store-bought puff pastry
120 g/1 stick plus 1 tsp butter, softened
150 g/¾ cup caster/superfine sugar
2 eggs
150 g/1½ cups ground almonds
650 g/23 oz. fresh apricots
  (about 16 apricots)
4 tbsp apricot jam/jelly or preserves,
  sieved

MAKES 12

Preheat the oven to 190°C (375°F) Gas 5. Roll the pastry out to form a rectangle measuring 35 x 25 cm/14 x 9¾ inches. Lay it out on a large, flat sheet pan and turn in 1 cm/¾ inch along each side towards the centre.

Beat the butter and sugar together in a large bowl and add the eggs. Beat until well mixed. Add the ground almonds and beat again, until the mixture is smooth. Spoon it onto the pastry, and spread it in an even layer with a spatula.

Cut the apricots in half and remove the pits. Arrange them (quite closely together) over the frangipane mixture. Transfer the sheet pan to the oven and bake for about 35–40 minutes, until the frangipane is firm and the apricots are softened and a little charred here and there. Remove from the oven and brush with the sieved jam/jelly. Cut into squares and serve warm or cold, with thickly whipped cream or icecream.

COCONUT MACAROON QUEEN OF PUDDINGS

200 g/7 oz. desiccated/
　dried shredded coconut
80 g/⅓ cup plus 1 tsp butter
50 g/¼ cup caster/superfine sugar
1 tsp vanilla bean paste
2 eggs, plus 1 egg yolk
300 g/10½ oz. raspberry or
　strawberry jam/jelly
3 egg whites
150 g/¾ cup caster/superfine sugar

a 30 x 17 x 2.5 cm/11¾ x 6¾ x 1 inch
　brownie pan, lightly greased and lined
　with baking parchment

SERVES 4–6

Queen of puddings is an old-fashioned British nursery pudding made of bread or cake crumbs cooked in an egg custard, topped with jam/jelly and crowned with meringue. I've swapped the traditional base for a chewy coconut macaroon mixture, which I think adds something deliciously different and rather special.

Preheat the oven to 170°C (325°F) Gas 3. Rub the coconut and butter together in a bowl until the butter has been evenly incorporated. Add the 50 g/¼ cup of sugar, the vanilla bean paste, eggs and egg yolk. Stir to combine. Spoon the mixture evenly into the prepared brownie pan and smooth over with a palette knife. Bake for 20 minutes, until golden and firm.

Spread the jam/jelly evenly over the coconut base.

Whisk the egg whites until firm and glossy. Gradually add the 150 g/¾ cup of sugar, whisking a little after each addition, until the sugar has been fully incorporated and the meringue is glossy and firm. Pipe or spoon it over the jam/jelly.

Return the brownie pan to the oven and bake for a further 20–25 minutes, until the meringue is golden brown and crisp. Serve warm or cold.

CHERRY, WHITE CHOCOLATE & RATAFIA BRIOCHE & BUTTER PUDDING

300 g/10½ oz. brioche
50 g/3½ tbsp butter, softened
250 g/9 oz. cherries, pitted
75 g/2¾ oz. white chocolate,
　roughly chopped
4 eggs
250 ml/1 cup plus 1 tbsp double/
　heavy cream
150 ml/⅔ cup whole milk
1 tsp vanilla bean paste
50 g/1¾ oz. ratafia biscuits or crisp
　amaretti biscuits, crumbled
cream or ice cream, to serve

a 30 x 17 x 2.5 cm/11¾ x 6¾ x 1 inch
　brownie pan, lightly greased and lined
　with baking parchment

SERVES 4–6

Speckled with juicy cherries and little nuggets of creamy white chocolate, this dreamy, crunchy-topped pudding is awesome. Dangerously so. But you're worth it, and so are the people you'll be sharing it with.

Preheat the oven to 170°C (325°F) Gas 3. Cut the brioche into 1 cm/⅜ inch slices (no need to cut the crusts off), butter them on one side, and then cut each slice into quarters, diagonally. Arrange the brioche triangles across the base of the prepared brownie pan, standing them up slightly. Scatter the cherries and chopped white chocolate evenly over the top, pushing some of the cherries into the brioche here and there.

Beat the eggs, double/heavy cream, milk and vanilla bean paste together in a large bowl. Pour the mixture through a fine sieve, over the brioche and fruit.

Scatter the crumbled ratafia or amaretti biscuits evenly over the top of the pudding, and transfer to the oven. Bake for about 30 minutes, until the custard is lightly set and the topping is crisp and golden. Serve warm, with extra cream or ice cream.

FRAGRANT BLOOD ORANGE & ALMOND CAKE

150 g/1¼ sticks butter, softened
300 g/1½ cups caster/superfine sugar
60 g/scant ¼ cup honey
5 eggs
200 g/1⅓ cups semolina or
  fine polenta/cornmeal
100 g/1 cup ground almonds
½ tsp baking powder
4 blood oranges
4 tbsp marmalade, to glaze

a 30 x 17 x 2.5 cm/11¾ x 6¾ x 1 inch
  brownie pan, lightly greased and
  lined with baking parchment

MAKES 15

This fragrant cake doesn't contain any flour, which helps give it an irresistible, dense but light texture. You can use ordinary oranges, but blood oranges have such a beautiful colour when they're in season, it's really worth seeking them out.

Preheat the oven to 170°C (325°F) Gas 3. Whisk the butter and sugar together in a bowl until the mixture is really light and fluffy. Whisk in the honey and then add the eggs, one at a time, whisking between each addition, until the eggs are fully incorporated. If the mixture starts to look a little curdled, simply add some of the semolina and ground almonds. Stir in the remaining semolina (or polenta/cornmeal) and ground almonds, together with the baking powder. Grate the zest from two of the oranges and add this into the mixture, then spoon everything into the prepared brownie pan.

Top and tail the oranges, stand them on a cutting board and carefully slice away the peel, taking care to remove all of the pith as you do so. Thinly slice the oranges and arrange them lightly over the top of the cake mixture. Bake for about 35 minutes or so, until a skewer inserted into the centre of the cake comes out clean, and the cake is golden and springy in the centre. Remove from the oven.

Push the marmalade through a fine sieve to remove any peel, and brush it liberally over the hot cake. Leave the cake to cool completely, before cutting into squares to serve.

SWEET BAY-SCENTED COCONUT & LIME RISOTTO
WITH BLACKBERRIES & BROWN SUGAR

Carnaroli risotto rice and coconut milk are both favourite ingredients amongst my storecupboard staples, so making this splendid dessert is something I can usually do whenever the fancy takes me. I've paired it with inky blackberries and lime zest here, but you could happily vary the fruit to suit the season.

150 g/¾ cup carnaroli rice
3 x 400 ml/13½ fl. oz. cans full-fat
  coconut milk
50 g/¼ cup caster/superfine sugar
a pinch of salt
2 fresh bay leaves
2 tbsp dark muscovado sugar
200 g/1½ cups blackberries
zest of 1 lime

SERVES 4

Preheat the oven to 190°C (375°F) Gas 5. Put the rice into a deep sheet pan and stir in the milk, squashing any big lumps down with the tines of a fork. Don't worry about smaller lumps, they will amalgamate fully as the mixture cooks. Add the sugar, salt and bay leaves. Transfer the pan to the oven and bake for 35–40 minutes, until the rice is soft and creamy. Give everything a stir halfway through the cooking time and take care not to let it dry out (add a dash of water if it seems to need more liquid). Remove the pan from the oven and scatter over the muscovado sugar, swirling it gently with a fork to create a rippled effect. Scatter with the blackberries and lime zest, and serve.

BAY-SCENTED HASSELBACK ORCHARD FRUITS
WITH CINNAMON MAPLE GLAZE

Fresh bay leaves add a heavenly flavour and scent to this lovely dish. They make a really pretty dessert – perfect with a coconut or conventional rice pudding. Cut them using the chopstick trick outlined in the hasselback coquina squash recipe on page 109, but leave in the cores, or they will collapse during the cooking process – they're easy enough to remove later.

3 ripe, but firm pears
3 crunchy eating apples
100 ml/⅓ cup plus 1 tbsp maple syrup
1 tsp ground cinnamon
juice of 1 orange
about 15–20 fresh bay leaves
extra maple syrup, to serve (optional)

SERVES 4

Preheat the oven to 180°C (350°F) Gas 4. Peel the pears and apples, and cut them in half. Cut them into thin slices, without going all the way through – using the method for hasselback coquina squash given on page 109.

Stir the maple syrup, ground cinnamon and orange juice together and brush this over the fruit, making sure to get lots of the mixture in between the slices. Cut the bay leaves in half along their length from stalk to tip and gently push them in between some of the slices in the fruit. Cook for 25 minutes, basting halfway through, and then pouring over any leftover glaze 5 minutes before the end of the cooking time.

Drizzle with extra maple syrup to serve, if desired.

PEARS IN RED WINE & STAR ANISE

With its elegant star-shaped points, I think star anise has to be one of the prettiest spices I know. It's really popular in Chinese and Vietnamese cooking, but I love it in this simple oven-baked pear recipe, where its glorious aniseed flavour permeates sweetened red wine and gives the most heavenly flavour to the fruit. These pears are lovely, served warm, with a good non-dairy icecream.

6 ripe, but firm pears
550 ml/18½ fl. oz. red wine
150–200 g/¾–1 cup caster/
  superfine sugar
1 lemon
4–5 whole star anise

SERVES 6

Preheat the oven to 190°C (375°F) Gas 5. Peel the pears, cut them in half from the stalk to the base, and gently scoop out the cores with a melon baller, if you have one (a teaspoon is ok, if you don't, but it just won't be as neat). Arrange them over the base of a deep sheet pan. Pour the red wine into a bowl and stir in the sugar. Pour this over the pears. Remove the zest from the lemon in quite large pieces, using a vegetable peeler. Add this to the wine, with the star anise.

Cover the pears and wine with a piece of baking parchment and transfer them to the oven. Bake for about 30 minutes, until the pears are soft when tested with the point of a knife. Remove the sheet pan from the oven and transfer the pears to a serving dish. Keep warm. Return the sheet pan to the oven and cook for a further 20 minutes, until the wine has reduced and thickened. Pour this mixture over the pears and serve with a good non-dairy ice cream. There's no need to remove the star anise, as they will add a pretty touch.

AQUAFABA SUMMER FRUIT MERINGUES

I can imagine that some of you might wonder if I've lost the plot when I say that you can make beautiful meringues that don't contain any egg white, but simply use the water drained from a can of chickpeas. Well, I kid you not! A fairly recent discovery, the liquid whisks up to soft, stable peaks and has been given the name 'aquafaba' – which does translate as 'bean water', but sounds rather more majestic.

So – what a bonus – if you're opening a can of protein-packed chickpeas (or even cooking them yourself from scratch) for a savoury dish, you can make meringues for dessert with the water, and there's zero waste! Epic.

liquid from 1 x 400-g/14-oz. can chickpeas
100 g/¹/₂ cup caster/superfine sugar
4–6 scoops of dairy-free or plant-based
   ice cream, to serve
400 g/14 oz. mixed summer berries
mint leaves, to decorate

MAKES 4–6

Preheat the oven to 110°C (225°F) Gas ¹/₄. Pour the chickpea water into a large bowl and whisk until the mixture forms stiff peaks – as you would do if you were making an egg meringue. If you have whisked the mixture to the correct stage, you should be able to turn the bowl upside down and the mixture won't move. Add the caster/superfine sugar, about a quarter at a time, and whisk until stiff each time. Unlike egg whites, the chickpea water will not over-whip and collapse.

When the sugar is fully incorporated and the mixture very stiff, spoon it into 4–6 heaped circles on a large, flat sheet pan lined with baking parchment. Transfer the pan to the oven and cook for about 1¹/₂ hours so that the meringues are crisp and firm. Don't be tempted to increase the oven temperature – the meringues need a low heat in order to dry out.

Remove the meringues from the oven and leave to cool. Top each with a scoop of dairy-free or plant-based ice-cream and scatter over an assortment of summer berries. Decorate with mint leaves and serve.

INDEX

INDEX **143**

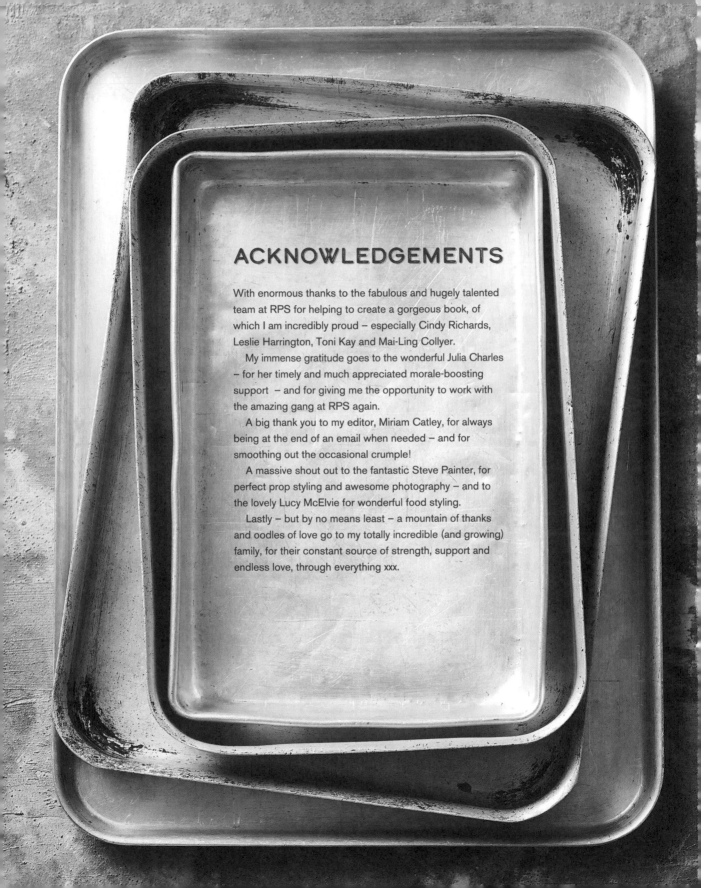

ACKNOWLEDGEMENTS

With enormous thanks to the fabulous and hugely talented team at RPS for helping to create a gorgeous book, of which I am incredibly proud – especially Cindy Richards, Leslie Harrington, Toni Kay and Mai-Ling Collyer.

My immense gratitude goes to the wonderful Julia Charles – for her timely and much appreciated morale-boosting support – and for giving me the opportunity to work with the amazing gang at RPS again.

A big thank you to my editor, Miriam Catley, for always being at the end of an email when needed – and for smoothing out the occasional crumple!

A massive shout out to the fantastic Steve Painter, for perfect prop styling and awesome photography – and to the lovely Lucy McElvie for wonderful food styling.

Lastly – but by no means least – a mountain of thanks and oodles of love go to my totally incredible (and growing) family, for their constant source of strength, support and endless love, through everything xxx.